FROEBEL AS A PIONEER IN MODERN PSYCHOLOGY

BY
E. R. MURRAY

Author of "A Story of Infant Schools and Kindergartens"

"Through the battle, through defeat, moving yet and never stopping. Pioneers! O Pioneers!"

Psychology Classics

PREFACE

Some day Froebel will come to his own, and the carefulness of his observation, the depth of his thought, the truth of his theories, and the success of his actual experiments in education will all be acknowledged.

There are few schools nowadays so modern as the short-lived Keilhau, with its spirit of freedom and independence and its "Areopagus" in which the boys themselves judged grave misdemeanours while the masters settled smaller matters alone. There are few schools now which have such an all-round curriculum, including, as it did, the mother tongue as well as classics and modern languages; ancient and modern history; Nature study and Nature rambles; school journeys, lasting for two or three weeks and extending as far as Switzerland for the older lads, while the younger boys visited German towns and were made acquainted with peasant life; definite instruction in field-work, in building and carpentry, etc.; religious teaching in which Middendorf endeavoured "to show the merits of the religions of all nations"; physical training with the out-of-doors wrestling ground and shooting stand and gymnasium "for every spare moment of the winter," and organized games; and dramatic teaching where "classic dramas" and other plays were performed, and for which the boys built the stage and painted the scenes. There was even co-education, "flirtation being unknown," because all had their heads so full of more important matters, but where free intercourse of boy and girl "softened the manners of the young German savages."

The purpose of this book is to show that all these things, besides the Kindergarten and the excellent plan for the Helba Institute, did not come into being by chance, but were the outcome of the deep reflection of a man who combined the scientific with the philosophic temperament; and who, because his ideal as a teacher was "Education by Development," had made a special study of the instinctive tendencies, and the requirements of different stages of child development, as I have tried to prove in Chapters VI and VII.

I should like to explain one or two points, first, that though for all quotations I have referred to the most commonly used translations of Froebel's writings, yet I have frequently given my own rendering when the other seemed inadequate; secondly, that I have endeavoured to give the context as often as possible, and have also given the actual German words, that I might not be accused of reading in modern ideas which are not really in the text; and, lastly, that I have purposely repeated quotations rather than give my readers the trouble of turning back to another page.

In conclusion may I take this opportunity of paying grateful thanks first to Miss Alice Words and to Miss K. M. Clarke, without whose kind encouragement I should never have completed my task, and also to Professor Alexander for several helpful suggestions, and to Miss Ida Sachs for friendly help.

E. R. Murray.

CONTENTS

EXPLANATION OF REFERENCES
To the Works of Froebel quoted in the text

E = EDUCATION OF MAN. TRANSLATED BY W. N. HAILMANN. M = MUTTER U. KOSE LIEDER. TRANSLATED BY F. AND E. LORD. P = PEDAGOGICS OF THE KINDERGARTEN. TRANSLATED BY JOSEPHINE JARVIS. L = LETTERS. \'7d TRANSLATED BY EMILIE MICHAELIS AND H. KEATLEY MOORE, B.A., B.MUS. A = AUTOBIOGRAPHY.

CHAPTER I
Froebel's Anticipation of Modern Psychology

"A great man condemns the world to the task of explaining him."

The purpose of this little book is to show that Froebel's educational theories were based on psychological views of a type much more modern than is at all generally understood. It is frequently stated that Froebel's psychology is conspicuous by its absence, but in a somewhat close study of Froebel's writings I have been again and again surprised to find how much Froebel seems to have anticipated modern psychology.

A probable reason for the overlooking of so much sound psychological truth is to be found in the fact that much of it is obscured by details which seem to us trivial, but which Froebel meant as applications of the theories he was endeavouring to make clear to minds not only innocent of, but incapable of, psychology.

Most educationists have read "The Education of Man," but few outside the Kindergarten world are likely to have bestowed much thought on Froebel's later writings. It is in these, however, that we see Froebel watching with earnest attention that earliest mental development which is now regarded as a distinct chapter in mental science, but which was then largely if not entirely ignored.

With the same spirit of inquiry and the same field for investigation—for children acted and thought then as they act and think now—it is only natural that Froebel should have made at least some of the same discoveries as the genetic psychologist of to-day.

It would be unfair at any date to expect a complete psychology from a writer whose subject is not mental science, but education. Mistakes, too, one must expect, and these are not to be ignored.[1] Still there remains a solid amount of psychological discovery for which Froebel has had as yet but little credit.

Indeed, just as his disciples have been inclined, like all disciples, to think that their master has said the last word on his own subject, so have opponents of Froebelian doctrines, irritated perhaps by these pretensions, made direct attacks on somewhat insufficient grounds. In a later chapter, an attempt has been made to deal with what seems unfounded in such attacks.[2]

The major part of the book, however, is intended to show the correctness of Froebel's views on points now regarded as of fundamental importance, and generally recognized as modern theories. For this purpose passages from Froebel's writings are here compared with similar passages from such undoubted authorities as Dr. James Ward, Professor Stout, Professor Lloyd Morgan, Mr. W. Macdougall, Mr. J. Irving King, and others.

In the first place, it should be noted that Froebel was fully aware of the necessity for a psychological basis for his educational theories.

Writing in 1841, he says:

"I am firmly convinced that all the phenomena of the child world, those which delight us, as well as those which grieve us, depend upon fixed laws as definite as those of the cosmos, the planetary system and the operations of Nature; it is therefore possible to discover them and examine them. When once we know and have assimilated these laws, we shall be able powerfully to counteract any retrograde and faulty tendencies in children, and to encourage, at the same time, all that is good and virtuous."—*L., p. 91.*

Nor was Froebel in any doubt as to how these laws are to be discovered, and his order of investigation is very similar to that prescribed by Professor Stout. The latter, though regarding genetic psychology as "the most important and most interesting," considers that it should be preceded by:—1, A general analysis of consciousness, analytic and largely introspective; 2, An investigation of the laws of mental process, "analytic also, inasmuch as we endeavour to ascertain the general laws of mental process by analysis of the fully developed mind."

Froebel, too, regards the analytic as a necessary preparation for the genetic, and says that parents and teachers, who wish to supply the needs of the child at different stages of development:

"are to consider life *firstly* through looking into themselves, into the course of their own development, its phenomena and its claims—through the retrospection (Rückblick) of the earliest possible years of their own lives, and also the introspection (Einblick) of their present lives, that their own experience may furnish a key to the problem of the child's condition (den Zustand des Kindes in sich zu lösen). *Secondly*, by the deepest possible search into the life of the child, and into what he must necessarily require according to his present stage of development."—*P., p. 168.*

Professor Stout adds later that anthropology and philology may ultimately yield results as important as those yielded by physiology. Froebel could have no idea of the physiological parallel to mental process, but he did not omit the anthropological inquiry, for in another passage he enlarges his first point, declaring that:

"It is essential for parents and teachers, for the sake of their children, and that their educational efforts may meet with a rich reward, not only to recall as far as possible the first phenomena, the course and conditions of the development of their own lives, but that they should compare this with the phenomena, the course and conditions of the development of the world, and of life in general in Nature and History, and so by degrees raise themselves to a knowledge of the general as well as of the particular laws of life development, that the guidance of the child may find in these laws a higher and stronger—their true foundation, as well as their surest determination."—*P., p. 66.*

Even his detractors generally allow that Froebel had a wonderful insight into child-nature, but this is too often spoken of as if it were due to some specialized faculty of intuition, not known to psychology.

Froebel's knowledge of child-nature came to him precisely as it comes to the psychologist of the present day, through patient observation of the doings of little children, and thoughtful interpretation of their possible meaning. It is true that he drew his conclusions from too narrow a field, but of this he was well aware. In a letter to a cousin thanking her for the "comparative account of the various manifestations of children," which she had sent him, he complains, *and this, be it remembered, in 1840,* that "it is a subject to which one can rarely get even cultivated parents to pay attention," and he adds:

"I would beg of you to collect as many observations for me as you can, both things which you yourself have observed, and also remarks made by your Robert and the other children when at play. If you have the time for this, pray do it for the furtherance of the cause; other friends are at work for me in the same way."—*L., p. 67.*

In another letter to this cousin he says:

"It would delight me greatly if you could confide to me what you remember of your feelings, perceptions, and ideas as a mother greeting the new-born life of her infant, and your observations of the first movements of its limbs and the beginning of the development of its senses."—*L., p. 110.*

To another friend he writes:

"In the interests of the children I have still another request to make—that you would record in writing the most important facts about each separate child. It seems to me most necessary for the comprehension, and for the true treatment of child-nature, that such observations should be made public from time to time, in order that children may become better and better understood in their manifestations, and may therefore be more rightly treated, and that true care and observation of unsophisticated childhood may ever increase."—*L., p. 89.*

Froebel made these requests, as he made his own observations, as the result of the conviction with which he declares himself "thoroughly penetrated,"

"that the movements of the young and delicate mind of the child, although as yet so small as to be almost unnoticeable, are of the most essential consequence to his future life."—*P., p. 53.*

"Why do we observe the child less than the germ of a plant? Is it to be supposed that in the child, the capacity to become a complete human being is contained less than in the acorn is contained the capacity to become a strong, vigorous and complete oak?"—*P., p. 62.*

"We cannot pass over unmentioned the fact, essential for the whole life of the child, for the whole course of his development, that phenomena and impressions which seem to us insignificant, and which we generally leave unnoticed, have for the child, and especially for his inner world, most important results, since the child develops more through what seems to us small and imperceptible, than through what appears to us large and striking ... hence—wholly contrary to prevailing opinion—nowhere is consideration of that which is small and insignificant of more importance than in the nursery."—*P., p. 125.*

Professor Dewey, one of the few important educational writers who do justice to Froebel as a pioneer, gives as a general summary of his educational principles:

"1. That the primary business of school is to train children in co-operative and mutually helpful living; to foster in them the consciousness of mutual interdependence, and to help them practically in making the adjustments that will carry this spirit into overt deeds.

"2. That the primary root of all educative activity is in the instinctive, impulsive attitudes and activities of the child, and not in the presentation and application of external material, whether through the ideas of others or through the senses; and that, accordingly, numberless spontaneous activities of children, plays, games, mimic efforts, even the apparently meaningless motions of infants—exhibitions previously ignored as trivial, futile, or even condemned as positively evil—are capable of educational use, nay, are the foundation-stones of educational effort.

"3. That these individual tendencies and activities are organized and directed through the uses made of them in keeping up the co-operative living already spoken of; taking advantage of them to reproduce on the child's plane the typical doings and occupations of the larger maturer society into which he is finally to go forth; and that it is through production and creative use that valuable knowledge is secured and clinched."[3]

So little, however, are these principles understood as Froebel's, that in the Pedagogical Seminary for July, 1900, a paper was published on "The Reconstruction of the Kindergarten," wherein it was maintained that the basis of reconstruction must be the child's natural instincts. The writer, Mr. Eby, had apparently no idea that the Kindergarten was originally based on this very foundation. He evidently did not know that Froebel has given, in his "Education of Man," a very fair account of these instincts, omitting nothing of great importance, and pointing, at least, to a better principle of classification than that adopted by Mr. Eby.[4] It is, however, only fair to Froebel to mention that he himself regarded his own account as far from being commensurate with the importance of the subject, for the year following that of the publication of "The Education of Man" he writes:

"Since these spontaneous activities of children have not yet been thoroughly thought out from a high point of view, and have not yet been regarded from what I might almost call their cosmical and anthropological side, we may from day to day expect some philosopher to write a comprehensive book about them."—*A., p. 76.*

The problems Froebel endeavoured to solve are precisely those which are absorbing the genetic psychologist of the present day, as stated, for example, in Mr. Irving King's "Psychology of Child Development," viz.: "to examine the various forms of the child's activity, to get some insight into the nature of the child himself"—"to get at the meaning of child-life in terms of itself."

Every reader of "The Education of Man" will remember how Froebel uses his own boyish reminiscences to help others to understand childish actions often utterly misunderstood. In his paper on "Movement Plays" he writes:

"In that nurture of childhood which is intended to assist development, it is by no means sufficient to supply play-material in proportion merely to the stage of development already outwardly manifest. It is at the same time of the utmost importance to trace out the inner process of development and to satisfy its demands.… In the nurture, development, and education of the child, and especially in the attempt to employ him, his own nature, his own life and energy must be the main consideration. The knowledge of isolated and external phenomena may occasionally be a guide-post pointing our direction, but it can never be a path leading to the specific aim of child culture and education; for *the condition of education is none other than comprehension of the whole nature and essence of humanity as manifested in the child.*"—*P., p. 239.*

Just as Mr. Irving King, writing in 1904, says that we must take as our starting-point the child's bodily activities, so did Froebel too declare, that:

"The present time makes upon the educator the wholly indispensable requirement—to comprehend the earliest activity, the first action of the child."—*P., p. 16.*

To this first action, Froebel devotes a whole paper, "Das erste Kindesthun," the opening sentence of which contains the words:

"As the new-born child, like a ripe grain of corn, bears life within itself which will be developed progressively and spontaneously, though in close connection with life in general, so activity and action are the first manifestations of awakening child-life."—*P., p. 23.*

Writing in 1847, Froebel says that "decision, zeal, and perseverance" must be brought to bear upon his plan, in order that:

"(*a*) More careful observation of the child, his relationships and his line of development, may become general amongst us; and thereby

"(*b*) A better grounded insight be obtained into the child's being, mental and physical, and the general collective conditions of his life.… Deeper insight will be gained into the meaning and importance of the child's actions and outward manifestations."—*L., p. 248.*

This quotation is important as showing that Froebel was deliberately looking for "*a line of development*," that he might better understand "the child's being, mental and physical." Considering that Froebel wrote between 1826 and 1850, the important points on which he may be said to have successfully anticipated modern psychology are, his recognition that the mind is what he calls "a tri-unity" of action, feeling, and thought; his treatment of early mental activity and his definition of will; his conception of the earliest consciousness as an undifferentiated whole; his recognition of the importance of action not only in the realm of perception, but also in that of feeling; and his surprisingly complete account of instinct. Such anticipations are due to the fact that the idea of development then new to the scientific world possessed his very soul.

"Humanity, *which lives only in its continuous development* and cultivation, seems to us dead and stationary, something to be modelled over again and again in accordance with its present type. We are ignorant of our own nature and the nature of humanity...."—*E., p. 146.*

"God neither ingrafts nor inoculates. He *develops* the most trivial and imperfect things in continuously ascending series and in accordance with eternal self-grounded and self-developing laws. And God-likeness is and ought to be man's highest aim in thought and deed."—*E., p. 328.*

Justice has already been done to Froebel's philosophy by Dr. John Angus MacVannel, who says in his closing paragraph:

"Froebel's system has that unmistakable mark of greatness about it that makes it worth our faithful effort to understand it, and turn its conclusions to our advantage.... His philosophy of education taken as a whole seems, perhaps, the most satisfactory we have yet had. One cannot but believe, however, that the candid reader will at times find conclusions in his writings sustained by reasonings, that are inadequately developed and important questions by no means satisfactorily answered.... On the other hand we must not forget that it is insight, rather than exactitude, that is the life of a philosophy; herein lies the secret of Froebel's lasting influence and power."[5]

CHAPTER II
Froebel's Analysis of Mind

It is probably due to the emphasis which Froebel laid upon the careful observation and equally careful interpretation of the very earliest manifestations of mental activity, that his views as to mental analysis approach so closely to more modern ideas. His psychology cannot possibly be dismissed as "faculty psychology" in which the mind of a child is regarded as a smaller and weaker replica of the mind of an adult. The older psychologies, Professor Stout points out, are based chiefly, if not entirely, on introspection alone, while Froebel, as we have already seen, demanded close observation of children in general, and of "each separate child," as well as consideration of mental development in the race, in addition to introspection.

This "too exclusive reliance upon introspection" to which Professor Stout refers as "the fundamental error" of the faculty psychology, caused the older writers to infer that just as a child is possessed of legs, arms and hands, smaller and weaker, but otherwise apparently the same as those of an adult, even so did he possess mental "faculties," such as memory and imagination, which, like the little legs and arms, only required exercise in order to grow strong. "It never occurred to them," writes Professor Stout, "that the powers of understanding, willing, imagining, etc., instead of existing at the outset, might have arisen as the result of a long series of changes, each of which paved the way for the next." It did more than "*occur*" to Froebel, it was a cardinal point with him. Professor Stout points out that the idea of development is essential to mental science, and Froebel was a biologist actually studying development, before he became a psychologist. He came to the study of mind prepared to find just such a series of changes.[6] In speaking of evolution in general, he says:

"Each successive stage of development does not exclude the preceding, but takes it up into itself, ennobled, uplifted, perfected."—*P., p. 198.*

He speaks of:

"the master thought, the fundamental idea of our time, that is, the education and development of mankind."—*L., p. 149.*

And in his "Education of Man," in a long and eloquent passage on the need for continuity of training from the tiniest of beginnings, he says:

"It is highly pernicious and even destructive to consider the stages of human development as distinct, and not as life shows them, continuous in themselves, in unbroken transitions."—*E., p. 27.*

The analysis of mind which Froebel recognizes, is the still commonly accepted "tripartite," but he never fails to refer to this as a unity or a tri-unity. Indeed, his constant harping upon this string becomes almost wearisome, in spite of the ingenuity with which he continually varies his terms.

"The early phenomenon of child-life, of human existence in childhood, is an activity, one with feeling and perception (Wahrnehmen)."—*P., p. 23.*

"That the nature of man shows itself early in the life of the child, as feeling, acting and representing, thinking and perceiving, and that in this tri-unity is included the whole of his life utterance and activity, we have said repeatedly, and it lies open for any one to notice."—*P., p. 122.*

Disguised as Love, Life, and Light, this trinity is made the connection of man, on the one side with Nature, on the other side with God. God—who is Life, Love, and Light, the All—shows Himself in Nature, in the universe as life (energy), in humanity as love, and in wisdom or in the spirit as light. Energy or life man shares with Nature; by love he is united with humanity; and by light or wisdom he is at one with God.

For his "gift plays" Froebel claims that they "take hold of the child in the tri-unity of his nature":

"As now each of the single plays separately considered takes hold of the child early, in the tri-unity of his nature, as doing, feeling, and thinking, so yet more do the employments as a whole."—*P., p. 56.*

And a forcible passage runs:

"Only if the child is treated through fostering his instinct for activity in the tri-unity of his nature, as living, loving, and perceiving, in the unity of his life, only thus can he develop as that which he is, the manifold and organized, but in himself single, whole."—*P., p. 12.*

This development of the threefold yet single nature constitutes the "harmonious development," reiterated *ad nauseam* and without explanation, in Kindergarten text-books. It is also the key to much that seems to us useless detail as to the toys and games of early childhood. The mother is told that:

"It is of the highest importance for the nurse to consider the earliest and slightest traces of the organization (Gliederung) within itself of the child's mind as bodily, emotional and intellectual, that in his development from mere existence to perception and thought, none of these directions of his nature should be fostered at the expense of the other ... the real foundation, the starting-point of human development is the heart and the emotions, but cultivation of action and thought (die Ausbildung zur That und zum Denken) must go side by side with it, constantly and inseparably: and thought must form itself into action, and action resolve and clear itself into thought; but both have their roots in the emotional nature."[7]—*P., p. 42.*

The first part of the following quotation from a letter written in 1851 towards the close of Froebel's life might almost be taken from a text-book of the present day:

"We find also three attitudes, spheres of work, and regions of mind in man:

"(1) the region of the soul, the heart, Feeling;

"(2) the region of the mind, the head, Intellect;

"(3) the region of the active life, the putting forth to actual deed, Will.

"As mental attitudes these three divisions seem the wider apart the more we contemplate them; as spheres of work and regions of mind they seem quite separate and perfect opposites. But the highest and most absolute opposition is that which most needs, and necessitates reconciliation; complete opposites condition their uniting link. The need for the uniting link appears in almost every circumstance of life.... To satisfy that need is the most imperative need now set before the human race, ... you will realize that the strengthening of character which we all agree to be a necessity of the age, is to be gained not only by stimulating and elevating the soul and the emotions, but by raising the whole mind, by training the intellect and the will.... Then the heart would acknowledge and esteem the intellectual power, just as the intellect already recognizes feeling as that which gives true warmth to our lives; and life as a whole would make manifest the soul which quickens existence, and gives it a meaning, as well as the intellect which gives it precision and culture. *Intellect, feeling* and *will* would then unite, *a many-sided power*, to build up and constitute our life. In the room of the unstable character which must result from the mere cultivation of the one department of emotion; in the room of the doubt, or, I might say empty negation, which too often proceeds from the mere cultivation of the intellect; in the room of the materialism, animalism, and sensuality which must come from the mere attention to the body, and physical side of our nature; we should then have the harmonious development of every side of our nature alike, we should then be able to build up a life which would be everywhere in touch with God, with physical nature, with humanity at large."—*L., p. 300.*

In his article in the Encyclopædia Britannica, Dr. Ward says, that in taking up the question of what we exactly mean by *thinking*, "we are really passing one of the hardest and fastest lines of the old psychology—that between sense and understanding. So long as it was the fashion to assume a multiplicity of faculties the need was less felt for a clear exposition of their connection. A man had senses and intellect much as he had eyes and ears; the heterogeneity in the one case was no more puzzling than in the other."

In this connection it can again be shown that Froebel was in advance of the old psychologists. In the first of the two games in the Mother-Play book dealing with sense-training —two out of forty-nine, the remainder dealing chiefly with action—he makes it very clear that he draws no hard and fast line between sense and understanding. He tells the mother that Nature speaks to the child through the senses, which act as gateways to the world within, but that light comes from the mind:

"Durch die Sinne, schliesst sich auf des Innern Thor Doch der Geist ist's der dies zieht ans Licht hervor."

And when he says that the baby in the cradle should not be left unoccupied if it wakes, he uses a pronoun in the singular in referring to "the activity of sense and mind." He suggests hanging a cage containing a lively bird in the child's line of vision and adds:

"This attracts the activity of the child's senses and mind and gives *it* nourishment in many ways."[8]—*E., p. 49.*

The faculty psychology and the formal discipline theory that came from it, says Professor Horne, did not admit the possibility of training one faculty, e.g. perception, by training another, e.g. reason, "it was not the mind that was trained, but its faculties."

It is, however, of the merest infant that Froebel uses such expressions as "the awakening power of thought," "the tenderest growth of mind," and tells the mother that he "shows trace of thought, and can draw conclusions." The ball is given to the baby to help him "to find himself in the midst of his perceptive, operative, and his comparing (thinking) activity."[9]—*P., p. 55.* Long years before this he had written of the teaching of drawing, "this instruction addresses itself to the senses, and through them to the power of thought."—*E., p. 294.*

"He who does not perceive traces of the future development of the child, who does not foster these with self-consciousness and wisdom, when they lie hidden in the depths and in the night, will not see them clearly, will not nourish them suitably, at least, not sufficiently, when they lie open before him."—*P., p. 58.*

Instead of ready-made faculties Froebel recognizes possibilities, conditions, which will remain possibilities if the necessary stimulus is not forthcoming, for in noting how the mother talks to her infant, though she is obliged to confess that there can be no understanding of her words, he says the mother's instinctive action is right:

"for that which will one day develop, and which must originate, begins and must begin when as yet nothing exists but the conditions, the possibility."—*P., p. 40.*

Elsewhere he asks:

"Is it to be supposed that in the child the capacity for becoming a complete human being is contained less than in the acorn is contained the capacity to become a strong, vigorous and complete oak?"—*P., p. 62.*

And he speaks of how the mother appeals to the infant as

"understanding, perceptive and capable, for where there is not the germ of something, that something can never be called forth and appear."—*P., p. 31.*

It is true that in the same passage in which he speaks of "the tenderest growth of mind," he does speak of mental powers (Geisteskräfte), as indeed every one does, but a few lines above he has spoken of "the cultivation of the mental power of the child in different directions."[10] Besides, the mental powers to which he here alludes, and which are to be awakened and fostered in the infant, are the powers "to compare, to infer, to judge, to think."—*P., p. 57.* Here, too, Froebel gives a description of what he means by memory, and it is clearly not a separate faculty considered apart from another faculty, viz. imagination:

"The plays carried on with the ball awaken and exercise the power of the child's mind to place again before himself mentally a vanished object, to see it mentally even when the outer perception is gone; these games awaken and practise the power of re-presenting, of remembering, of holding fast in remembrance an object formerly present, of again thinking of it; that is, they foster the memory."—*P., p. 57.*

So even the infant is to think, and the progress is well described in the Mother Plays as "from experience of a thing, joined with thought about it, up to pure thought."—*M., p. 121.*

In a lecture[11] given many years ago, Dr. Ward sought to drive home to teachers the futility of this hard and fast line between sense training and training to think. And there are some interesting parallels between Dr. Ward's metaphors here and Froebel's writing in "The Education of Man." Dr. Ward said:

"Training of the senses, as it is not very happily called, is, if it is anything, so much intellectual exercise.… And nothing can be more absurd than to suppose it is not necessary.… By a judicious training in observation you begin to make a child think when it is five years old. … If a child is to think to any purpose, he must think as he goes on; as soon as the material he has gathered begins to oppress him he must think it into shape, or it will tend to smother intellectual life at its dawn, as a bee is drowned in its own honey, for want of cells in which to store it."

It is in describing how the little child collects pebbles, twigs, leaves, etc., that Froebel writes:

"The child loves all things that enter his small horizon and extend his little world. To him the least thing is a new discovery; but it must not come dead into the little world, nor lie dead therein, lest it obscure the small horizon and crush the little world.… It is the longing for interpretation that urges the child to appeal to us … the intense desire for this that urges him to bring his treasures to us and lay them in our laps."—*E., p. 73.*

The help we are told to give at first is merely to supply the child with a name, for "through the name the form is retained in memory and defined in thought." Later the mother is told to provide "encouragement and help, that the child may weave into a whole what he has found scattered and parted." As a type of the help considered necessary we have:

"'Mother, are the pigeons and hens birds, for the pigeons live in pigeon-houses and the chickens don't fly?' 'Have they no feathers, child; have they no wings? Haven't they two legs like all birds?' 'Are the bees and butterflies and beetles birds, too: for they have wings and fly much higher.…' 'Look, they have no feathers, they build no nests.'"—*M., p. 56.*

In another passage Froebel calls it not only advisable but necessary that the parents, without being pedantic or over-anxious, should connect the child's doings with language, because this "increases knowledge, and awakens that judgment and reflection (die Urtheilskraft und das Nachdenken), to which man, left to Nature, does not attain sufficiently early."—*E., p. 79.*

Giving names, and helping in classification is surely a sufficient parallel to Dr. Ward's "thinking the material into shape," and just as the latter says that by such training you can "make a child think" when it is five years old, so Froebel in his chapter on "Man in Earliest Childhood" makes his ideal father "sum up his rule of conduct in a few words," declaring that: "To lead children early to think, this I consider the first and foremost object of child-training."—*E., p. 87.*

Froebel's theories, then, cannot be dismissed as based on "faculty psychology," since it seems clear that wherever he found them his views on mental analysis were very similar to those now generally accepted. It is more remarkable, however, that he should have modern views about Conation and Will.

CHAPTER III
Will and its Early Manifestations

It is open to doubt whether any modern psychologist has yet given a better definition of fully developed Will than that given by Froebel eighty-seven years ago:

"Will is the mental activity of man ever consciously proceeding from a definite point, in a definite direction, to a definite conscious end and aim, in harmony with the whole nature of humanity."—*E., p. 96.*

With this definition compare what Professor Stout has to say:

"In its most complex developments, mental activity takes the form of self-conscious and deliberate volition, in which the starting-point is the idea of an end to be attained, and the desire to attain it; and the goal is the realization of this end, by the production of a long series of changes in the external world … it belongs to the essence of will, not merely to be directed towards an end, but to ideally anticipate this and consciously aim at it."[12]

Between these two definitions the difference is in the omission in Froebel's definition of any mention of desire, and this is supplied a little later, when, having stated that "by school here is meant neither the schoolroom, nor school-keeping, but the conscious communication of knowledge for a definite purpose, and in definite connection," he ends up with:

"By this knowledge, instruction and the school are to lead man *from desire to will*, from activity of will to firmness of will, and thus continually advancing, to the attainment of his destiny, of his earthly perfection."—*E., p. 139.*

Now Professor Stout's whole psychology is founded on his conception of mental activity. Towards the end of his second volume he says: "The reader is already familiar with my general doctrine. It has pervaded the whole treatment of psychological topics in this work. The aim of the present chapter is to present it in a more systematic form, and to guard it against objections. Our starting-point lies in the conception of mental activity as the direction of mental process towards an end."

It is distinctly significant, therefore, to find how closely Froebel's ideas on the subject resemble Professor Stout's conception of mental activity.

"Conscious process," writes Professor Stout, "is in every moment directed towards an end, whether this end be distinctly or vaguely recognized by the conscious subject, or not recognized at all."

Froebel writes:

"In all activity, in every deed of man, even as a child, yes the very smallest, an aim is expressed, a reference to something, to the furthering or representing of something; … thus the child strives, even if unconsciously, to make his inner life objective, and through that perceptible, that so he may become conscious of it."—*P., pp. 237-240.*

The same idea, that conscious process is directed to an end, though there may be no consciousness of that end, is given in another passage, where Froebel is speaking of the need for satisfying a child's normal desire for playthings.

"Very often the child seeks for something, nevertheless he himself does not know at all what he seeks; at another time he puts something away from him and again knows not why."—*P., p. 168.*

Of the earliest mental activity Professor Stout writes:

"In its earliest and simplest form, mental activity consists in those simple reactions which without being determined by any definite idea of an end to be realized, tend on the whole to the maintenance of immediate pleasure and the avoidance of immediate pain."

The movements of the organism at this earliest stage "seem primarily adapted to the conservation and furtherance of vital process in general."[13]

Froebel speaks of the child's efforts:

"to put far from him that which is opposed to the needs of his life and yet would break in upon it."—*P., p. 167.*

He tells the mother that, in the first stages at least, the restlessness and tears of the infant will warn her of the presence of anything in his surroundings hurtful to his development, while his laughter and movements of pleasure will show "what according to the feeling of the child is suited to the undisturbed development of his life as an immature human being."

Mr. Stout goes on to say that such simple reactions are adapted "secondarily and by way of necessary corollary to the conservation and furtherance of conscious life." He tells us that: "The primary craving with which the education of the senses begins, so far as it does not involve such practical needs as that of food, may be described as a general craving for stimulation or excitement … this conation being in the first instance in the highest degree indeterminate."

Froebel, who speaks of the nurse "soothing the restless child *vaguely striving* for definite and satisfactory outward activity," tells us that:

"if his bodily needs are satisfied and he feels himself well and strong, the first spontaneous employment of the child is spontaneous taking in (selbstthätiges Aufnehmen) of the outer world."—*P., p. 29.*

He writes to Madame Schmidt, the cousin for whose assistance he has begged in observing children:

"This spontaneous activity of limb and vividness of sensation natural to infancy, and I may say inseparable from it, must also be carefully studied."—*L., p. 110.*

And, in the Mother Songs, he says:

"You can see how his bodily activity, the movement and use of his limbs, like the activity of his senses, all turn towards one point: Life must be grasped, experienced and perceived … he wants to appropriate the outer and to re-embody it … his susceptibility for all that gives and takes up life will strike you as something that elevates his life in every way; even as young plants and animals are susceptible to the faintest workings of light and warmth, or the impressions of their environment, however delicate. Moreover, this receptivity is most closely related to great general excitability and sensibility (Erregbarkeit, Reizbarkeit)."—*M., pp. 119-121.*

Froebel's views as to the nature both of early and of later mental activity then bear a strong resemblance to the modern view as stated by Professor Stout.[14]

In searching Froebel's writings to find what he has to say about the stages lying between early mental activity and fully developed will, between what he calls "natural activity of the will, and true genuine firmness of will," it soon becomes clear that it is impossible to separate what is said about will development, from what is said about intellectual development.[15] This is a natural consequence of Froebel's constant insistence on the unity of consciousness, and it is the position of modern psychology, whether written from the analytic or the genetic point of view. Mr. Irving King writes: "The functional point of view emphasizes first of all the intimate inter-relation of all forms of mental activity and the impossibility of describing any one aspect of consciousness except with reference to consciousness as a whole." Professor Stout, in his "Analytic Psychology," has a section entitled "Conation and Cognition developed coincidentally,"[16] while Froebel says:

"Thought must form itself in action, and action resolve and clear itself in thought."—*P., p. 42.*

Froebel speaks of his projected institution at Helba as "fundamental,"

"inasmuch as in training and instruction it will rest on the foundation from which proceed all genuine knowledge and all genuine practical attainments; it will rest on life itself and on creative efforts, *on the union and interdependence of doing and thinking*, representation and knowledge, art and science. The institution will base its work on the pupil's personal efforts in work and expression, making these, again, the foundation of all genuine knowledge and culture. Joined with thoughtfulness, these efforts become a direct medium of culture."—*E., p. 38.*

Professor Stout's account of how the unconscious mental activity of early childhood becomes transformed into the definite and conscious activity of fully developed will is, stated briefly, something to this effect. It is of the essence of conation to seek its own satisfaction, and this is only possible as the conation becomes definite. "Blind craving gives place to open-eyed desire," as the original conation tends to define itself. So "the gradual acquisition of knowledge through experience is but another expression for the process whereby the originally blind craving becomes more distinct and more differentiated." The grouping of cognitions is not produced by the conscious needs: "It is the way in which the conation itself grows and develops."

For this account we can find a wonderfully exact parallel in one of Froebel's less well-known papers, that on "Movement Plays."

"All outer activity of the child has its ultimate and distinctive foundation in his inmost nature and life. The deepest craving of this inner activity is to behold itself mirrored in some outward object. In and through such representation, the child himself grasps and perceives the nature, direction and aim of his own activity, and learns also further to regulate and determine his life, that is his activity, according to these outward phenomena."—*P., p. 238.*

This craving for outward representation, by satisfaction of which the child gains knowledge of the ends of his activity, is an exact equivalent of Stout's blind craving which gives place to open-eyed desire as it tends to define itself. Froebel's conclusion, that only as this unconscious or blind craving for action is satisfied does the child become "conscious of the nature, direction and ends of his own activity," is but another way of stating Professor Stout's conclusion, that the grouping of cognitions, which is the gradual acquirement of knowledge through experience, is "the way in which the conation itself grows and develops." So, cognition and conation are developed simultaneously, or, to repeat Froebel's own phrase, "Thought forms itself in action, and action resolves and clears itself in thought."

Professor Stout goes on to say that in this defining process one conation springs out of another, whereby as one conation is satisfied and so comes to an end, another becomes in its turn the end of activity. He takes as illustration the child learning to walk, saying, "The mental attitude of the child learning to walk is one of conscious endeavour. When he has become habituated to the act, he performs it without attending to his movements, his mind being fixed on the attainment of other ends." Froebel proceeds in the same way, using the very same example. He has already said that at first the child:

"cares for the use of his body, his senses and limbs, merely for the sake of their use and practice, but not for the sake of the results of this use. He is wholly indifferent to this; *or, rather, he has as yet no idea whatever of this*."—*P., p. 48.*

Now, in the paper on movement, he goes on:

"Each sure and independent movement gives the child pleasure, because of the feeling of power which it arouses in him. Even simple walking produces this effect, for it gives the child a threefold feeling, a threefold consciousness: First, the consciousness that he *moves* himself; secondly, that he moves himself from one place to another; third, that through this movement he attains or reaches something.... It is a well-established fact that his first walking gives the child pleasure as an expression of his power. *To this pleasure, however, are soon added the two joy-bringing perceptions of coming to something, and of being able to attain something.* These several perceptions should all be fostered at the same time ... he should get his limbs, and indeed his whole body, into his own power. He should learn to use his bodily strength and the activity of his limbs for definite purposes.... *The effort to reach a particular object may have its source in the child's desire to hold himself firm and upright by it, but we also observe that it gives him pleasure to be actually near the object, to touch it, to feel it, to grasp it, and perhaps also— which is a new phase of activity—to be able to move it.* Hence we see that the child when he has reached the desired object, hops up and down before it, and beats on it with his little arms and hands, in order, as it were, to assure himself of the reality of the object and to notice its qualities. It is well, *while the child is making these experiments*, to name the object and its parts. *The object of giving these names is not primarily the development of the child's power of speech, but to assist his comprehension of the object*, its parts and its properties, *by defining his sense-impressions."—P., p. 241.*

Another passage runs:

"The present effort of mankind is an endeavour after freer self-development.... Therefore the more or less clear aim of the individual is to attain to clearness about himself and about life, to comprehension and right use of life, to both insight and accomplishment.... Therefore the educator must understand the earliest activity and encourage the impulse to self-culture, through independent doing, observing and experimenting."—P., p. 16.

To say that a conation tends to define itself is only to say that unconscious ends tend to be replaced by conscious ends, and we have seen that both Froebel and Professor Stout give unconsciousness or consciousness of the end, as the difference between earlier and later forms of mental activity. Professor Stout's conclusion is that "apart from the perpetual germination of one conation out of another, the characteristic features of the mental life of human beings would be inexplicable."

Now, to be conscious of one's ends or aims is, in a certain sense, to be self-conscious, so the transition from earlier to later forms of mental activity is practically the development of self-consciousness. It is interesting, therefore, to see that just as Professor Stout gives as his explanation of human life, the perpetual germination of one conation out of another, so Froebel gives as his explanation, his meaning of life, the gradual development of self-consciousness.

Self-consciousness, involving true volition, or self-determination, is to Froebel "the end of man, for which he first was planned." It is, as he constantly put it, man's "destination."

"To become clearly conscious of all the conditions and relations in which and by means of which man exists makes man first become man in consciousness and in action."—P., p. 12.

"For man is destined for consciousness, for freedom, for self-determination."—E., p. 136.

"Self-consciousness belongs to the nature of man, is one with it; to become conscious of itself is the first task in the life of the child as a human being, as it is the task of his whole life."—P., p. 40.

"Who amongst us," exclaims Professor Royce, "conceives himself in his uniqueness except as the remote goal of some ideal process of coming to himself and of awakening to the truth about his own life? Only an infinite process can show me who I am."[17]

Froebel never loses sight of this. In his Autobiography he tells how he began "unwillingly" to write something in the album of a friend who was the owner of a beautiful farm, and he concludes: "Then my thoughts grew clear and I continued, 'Thou givest man bread; let my aim be to give man himself.'" That he verily believed that the gradual development of self-consciousness is the first task in the life of the child is abundantly evident. In the very beginning of his Mother Songs he tells the mother to give her child something to push against, "to bring the child to self-knowledge as soon as possible," and at the end he says, "When a child or human being has found himself and has firm hold over himself, he is ready to walk joyfully through life."

In "The First Action of a Child," Froebel writes:

"The nature of man, as man, is that he is self-conscious, and this is stamped with distinctness enough to be observed in the quite peculiar character of childish activity,[18] in his impulse to busy himself self-actively, spontaneously: an impulse which awakens simultaneously with mind, and which is in harmony with feeling and perception. If this tendency to spontaneous activity is fostered, man's triune nature—energy, emotion and intellect—is satisfied."—*P., p. 21.*

A realization of what Sir Oliver Lodge calls "the universal struggle for self-manifestation and corporeal realization, which plays so large a part in all activity," underlies all that Froebel has to say of the progress from unconscious activity to self-conscious volition. His view of the Universe is exactly that tentatively suggested by Professor Lodge, viz. that something akin to this universal struggle "is exhibited in a region beyond and above what is ordinarily conceived of as 'Nature.' The process of evolution can be regarded as the gradual unfolding of the Divine Thought or Logos, throughout the universe, by the action of Spirit upon matter."

This takes us out of the region of psychology, but Froebel's subject was not psychology, *per se*, but child development, as a part of the whole plan of evolution, man being the most highly developed of creatures.

The whole universe is an expression of the Divine, but man alone can become conscious of his origin.

"All things are destined to reveal God in their external and transient being…. It is the special destiny of man, as an intelligent and rational being to become conscious of his divine essence and to render this active, to reveal it in his life, with self-determination and freedom."—*E., p. 2.*

"Made in the image of God," meant to Froebel self-conscious and self-determined. The relation of man to God is expressed by Froebel as the relation of the thought to the thinker "*could the thought but become conscious of itself.*" In a letter of 1843, he says:

"At the basis of the Kindergarten lies an idea which serves alike for all the interstellar spaces, for all systems of the sun; the fulfilment of the divine will and the manifestation of the same. *In order to become such a manifestation of the divine, man has first to attain the basis of self-consciousness*; to which end serves the early culture of the spirit of humanity in the world of childhood."—*L., p. 133.*

In a paper entitled "A Second Review of the Plays," which really deals chiefly with evolution, we read:

"We must see clearly the conditions of development in Nature and then employ them in life. Thus only can we raise man upon his own plane, that is, the spiritual plane, at least to such a degree of perfection as is shown on their plane by the types of Nature.

"Man—the all-surveying—must develop himself by gradual growth of consciousness, must raise himself eventually to clear consciousness of the foundation, conditions and goal of his life."—*P., p. 198.*

It was as clear to Froebel as to Professor Lloyd Morgan that the lower animals are kept from reaching self-consciousness by the definiteness of their instincts,[19] but to Froebel as to Browning "in completed Man begins anew a tendency to God." Like Browning again, Froebel finds that man has "somewhat to cast off, somewhat to become," he, too, "finds Progress man's distinctive mark alone, not God's, and not the beasts'; God is, they are, man partly is, and wholly hopes to be."

"Man in his first period of life on earth is to be regarded while a child in three separate relations, which are united in themselves.

"(*a*) As a child of Nature, that is according to his earthly and natural conditions and connections, and in this relation bound, chained, unconscious, subject to impulses (als ein gebundenes, gefesseltes, unbewusstes, den Trieben unterworfenes).

"(*b*) As a child of God, and in this relation as a free being, destined to self-consciousness.

"(*c*) As a child of Humanity, and in this relation, as a being struggling from bondage toward freedom, toward consciousness."—*P., p. 11.*

And the beginning of all he finds in "The First Action of the Child." In the paper to which he gives this title Froebel writes:

"Helplessness and personal will, a mind of one's own, soon become therefore the turning-points of child-life, the fulcrum of which is free spontaneous activity, self-employment."—*P., p. 27.*

It is because Froebel believes this, that we hear so much of creative activity. Consciousness, which Meredith calls "the great result of mortal suffering," is the outcome of all the unconscious striving.

"The child, although unconsciously, strives to make his life outwardly objective, and thus perceptible and so to become conscious of it."—*P., p. 240.*

"Man only comes to the power of self-examination and self-knowledge in any relation whatever with the greatest difficulty, and must first learn to study himself … in the mirror of Nature and of all creation."—*L., p. 57.*

"The child must perceive and grasp his own life in an objective manifestation before he can perceive and grasp it in himself. Such mirroring of the inner life, such making of the inner life objective, is essential, for through it, the child comes to self-consciousness and learns to order, determine and master himself."—*P., p. 238.*

Froebel realizes then, that true volition is the outcome of unconscious striving, that it can only come through action, and, what is most important, through action which is the outcome of feeling, "worthy his effort." So, while stating that the formation of "a pure, strong and enduring will" is the main object of education, he takes care to point out that unless the boy is allowed to carry out in action "that which is within," ideas which have appealed to him, and which he has already made his own, that main object will not be easily attainable.

"To raise activity of will to firmness of will, and so to arouse, and form a pure, strong and enduring will, for the representation of a characteristic humanity, is the chief aim, the main object of the school…. The starting-point of all mental activity in the boy should be energetic and healthy, the direction should be simple and definite, the aim certain and conscious, and worthy of his effort. Therefore to raise the natural activity of the will to true genuine firmness of will, all the boy's activities should have reference to the development and accomplishment of what is within him. Activity of will proceeds from activity of the feelings, and firmness of will from firmness of the feelings, and where the first is lacking, the second will be difficult of attainment."—*E., p. 96.*

CHAPTER IV
Characteristics of the Earliest Consciousness

It is in the emphasis he lays upon the mental activity of the child from the very first, that Froebel approaches so closely to the position of the modern psychologist, and in his account of the earliest consciousness he distinctly resembles Professors Ward and Stout.

Only to "some of our most distinguished modern psychologists" does Professor Stout attribute a strong disposition to recognize in the elementary processes of perception and association, the rudimentary presence of these mental operations which in their higher form we call reasoning and constructive imagination.

Now Froebel writes:

"One can recognize and watch, even in the first stages of childhood, though only in their slightest traces and tenderest germs, all the mental activities which certainly do not stand out prominently till later life. Say not, ye parents, How can such tendencies lie already in the life of the child still so unconscious and so helpless? If they did not lie in it they could never be developed from it … for where there is not the germ of something, this something will never be called forth and appear.… As man is a being intended for increasing self-consciousness, so shall he also become an inferring and judging being (schliessendes und urtheilendes). Man has also a quite characteristic power of imagination, and—what must never be forgotten, but continually kept before the eyes as important and guiding—the new-born child not only will become man, but the man with all his qualities, and with the unity of his being, already appears and indeed is in the child."—*P., pp. 30-49.*

Psychologists in general, says Professor Stout, show a tendency, which he regards as erroneous, "to ignore the constructive aspect of early mental process, to recognize mental productiveness only in complete and advanced stages of mental development."

But Froebel, in speaking of the mother's play with a mere infant, when the coloured ball may present "the perception of an object as such," most distinctly states that the child's "first impressions, as it were the first cognitions," come to him in these early plays by *means of his own activity*, an activity of body emphatically, as we shall see presently, but an activity also of mind, of perception, "durch Wahrnehmen … durch dunkles Auffassen … durch Selbst-thätigkeit."[20]

Froebel uses such expressions as "the spontaneous reception" and even "the critical reception of the outer world," just as Dr. Ward, in refusing to recognize an internal sense, says "the new facts … are due to our mental activity, and not to a special mode of what has been called our sensitivity."

The active, rather than the passive attitude, strikes Froebel so forcibly that he calls the two modes of consciousness, the receiving of, and reacting upon impressions, a "double expression."

"The first voluntary needs of the child, if its bodily needs are satisfied and it feels well and strong, are observation of its surroundings, spontaneous reception of the outer world (selbstthätiges Aufnehmen der Aussenwelt) and play, which is spontaneous expression, or acting out of what is within. This double expression (Diese Doppeläusserung) of taking in and expressing outwardly is necessarily grounded in its nature, as in human nature in general; since the child's first earthly destiny is to attain by critical reception (durch prüfende Aufnahme) of the outer world into itself, by manifold inward impressions and outward expressions of its inner world, and by critical comparison of both, to the recognition of their unity...."—*P., p. 29.*

Professor Stout attributes this ignoring by certain psychologists of the constructive aspect of early mental process to a false view of the nature both of association and of construction, the fundamental fallacy of the associationists lying in their disposition to explain the nature and existence of a whole by reference to the nature and existence of the parts which are contained in it, so that "the parts must be supposed to pre-exist before they are combined, and to pre-exist in such a way that they need only to be in some manner externally brought together or associated in order to constitute the whole which contains them."

In like manner Dr. Ward accuses psychologists of having "usually represented mental advance as consisting fundamentally in the combination and recombination of various elementary units, the so-called sensations and primitive movements, or, in other words, in a species of mental chemistry."

That Froebel seems to have avoided the error thus pointed out by those two psychologists, is surprising enough, but it is even more surprising to find that this is probably due to the fact that his conception of the earliest possible consciousness is very much like theirs.

In rejecting "the atomistic view," Professor Ward maintains that "the further we go back, the nearer we approach to a total presentation, having the character of one general continuum in which differences are latent."

Froebel's account, as given in "The Education of Man," is very similar:

"Although in itself made up of the same objects and of the same organization, the external world comes to the child at first, out of its void, as it were, in misty, formless indistinctness, in chaotic confusion, even the child and the outer world merge into one another."—*E., p. 40.*

This description reminds us of Professor James' picturesque expression, "big, blooming, buzzing confusion," which is so often quoted, but which does not really convey so true a picture as Dr. Ward's account, for where there is no distinction there can surely be no confusion. But a few pages further on we find Froebel describing the infant consciousness before speech begins, as "*still an unorganized, undifferentiated unity*" (noch eine ungegliederte mannigfaltigkeitslose Einheit). This is identical with the expression used by Professor Stout, who, in speaking of the stage to which he gives the name "implicit apprehension," the apprehension of an unanalysed whole, uses the phrase "distinctionless unity." Froebel talks of the child feeling himself a whole and "so also, though unconsciously, seeking to grasp a whole, never merely a part as such." And just as Dr. Ward claims for psychology as well as for biology "what may be called a principle of progressive differentiation or specialization," so Froebel writes:

"The child mind develops according to the law which governs world development, viz.: that of progression from the unlimited to the limited, from the general to the special, from the whole to the part."—*P., p. 170.*

In this, of course, lies the reason for Froebel's correct apprehension of the infant mind, he was biologist first, and his mind was full of the idea of development.

"At the same time there begins in the child, as in the seed-corn, a development towards complexity."—*P., p. 172.*

"Whether we are looking at a seed or an egg, whether we are watching feeling or thought, what is definite proceeds everywhere from what is indefinite and this is the way in which your child's life is sure to show itself."—*M., p. 121.*

Professor Ward goes on to discuss what is implied in this process of differentiation or mental growth, saying that if analogies are to be taken from the physical world at all, the growth of a seed or embryo, will furnish far better illustrations of the unfolding of the contents of consciousness than the building up of molecules.

It was the endeavour, and quaint enough it seems to us, to translate this psychological truth into educational practice, that led Froebel to lay so much stress on the fact that the earliest of his so-called "Gifts" are indivisible wholes:

"Let us place ourselves at the nursery table, and try to perceive what the child is impelled to do in the beginning of his self-employment. Let us sit ourselves as unnoticed as possible considering how the child, after he has examined the self-contained tangible object in its form and colour, has moved it here and there and proved its solidity, how he then tries to divide it, at least to change its form…. Thus *after perception of the whole, the child desires to see it separated* into parts…. Let us stop at this significant phenomenon and try to discern through it what plaything following on the self-contained ball, hard and soft, and the solid hard cube, we should for inner reason and without arbitrariness give to the child."—*P., p. 117.*

Then come directions as to the manner in which the toy is to be presented:

"in order to give the child *the impression of the whole* (den Eindrück des Ganzen). *From this as the first fundamental perception* (der ersten Grundanschauung) *everything proceeds and must proceed.*"[21]

Starting from the conception of an undifferentiated totality or objective continuum, Dr. Ward says, "Of the very beginnings of this continuum we can say nothing, absolute beginnings are beyond the pale of science. Actual presentation consists in this continuum being differentiated; every differentiation constitutes a new presentation. Hence the common-place of psychologists: 'We are only conscious as we are conscious of change.'" …

As to absolute beginnings, Froebel too writes that these are past finding out, but he does so in order to call the mother's attention to the importance of the very earliest steps:

"Do not say, It is much too early…. Too early? Do you know when, where and how your child's intellectual development begins? Can you tell when and where is the boundary of existence that has not yet begun, and of its actual beginning, and how this boundary manifests itself?"—*M., p. 154.*

Coming now to what Froebel has to say as to how his "unorganized unity" becomes differentiated, we shall not find that his brief account differs in any really fundamental way from that of Professor Ward. Some of his expressions have a very modern sound, such as: "how the outer world begins to divide and analyse itself"; how "out of the indefinite outside and around the child comes the definite"; or again how the child gains "the three great perceptions of object, space and time, which at first were one collective perception." ("Die drei grossen Wahrnehmungen von Gegenstand, Raum und Zeit; welche anfangs in einer Gesammtwahrnehmung in dem Kinde ruhten.")—*P., p. 37.*

Commenting upon the phrase "We are only conscious as we are conscious of change,"

Dr. Ward remarks that the word change does not sufficiently explain what happens in differentiation, for this implies that the increased complexity is due to the persistence of former changes; such persistence being essential to the very idea of growth or development.... At the same time he is careful to point out that neither in "retentiveness" nor in assimilation is there "any confronting of the old with the new," any "active comparison." Without change of impression consciousness would be a blank, but "a difference between presentations is not at all the same as the presentation of that difference. The former must precede the latter; the latter, which requires active comparison, need not follow ... we must recognize objects before we can compare them."

Froebel says that:

"All the development of the child has its foundation in almost imperceptible attainments and perceptions ... the first perceptions, in the beginning almost imperceptible and evanescent, are fixed, increased and clarified by innumerable repetitions, and *by change*."—*P., p. 38.*

Froebel, too, goes back to this very earliest stage, the stage when a baby "begins to notice." He says that this indication of an intellect (Seelenaeusserung) begins when the child is a few weeks old, and is occasioned at first by the movement, that is change in position, of a bright object, "in and by means of the motion the child first perceives the object."—*P., p. 64.*

In another passage Froebel speaks of change as "a dim conception of sequence, and thus of dim comparison."

"These first impressions come to the child by means of perception and seeing, and by means of coming, staying and vanishing (of the ball); *by means of change*, thus also, in a certain point of view by means of early dim conceptions of sequence, of foundation and result, of cause and effect, and thus of dim comparison."—*P., p. 65.*

A change or difference which does not imply active comparison, and a change or sequence which does imply dim comparison are not very far apart, and Froebel makes his meaning clearer still by using the words "unconsciously comparing" (unbewusst vergleichend).

"By this play his attention is called to the precise shape of the cube; and he will look at it sharply, unconsciously comparing it with the hand, to which his eyes were first attracted."—*P., p. 84.*

Nor does Froebel omit to notice the necessary close connection of the new with the old, which Dr. Ward emphasizes.

"The child very often seeks for something without at all knowing what he seeks; in like manner he repels something without at all knowing why. Yet the child does not for this reason turn away accidentally, neither does he seek the accidental. Generally it is the new for which the child seeks, but not a novelty which has no connection with what has hitherto been, for that, should it appear, would obstruct development. He seeks the new which has developed from the old, like a bud from a branch. He seeks a new unexpected turn, a new unexpected use of a thing, new unexpected properties, new and yet unconsciously anticipated development, a new unexpected connection with his life.... The child indeed seeks for the new that is outside of himself, but not on account of its externality. Really he is seeking the new of which he feels premonitions in himself, in his own development. Since, however, he does not yet know this, and so cannot give an account of it, *the child seeks especially for change*, in order to gain a means of growing up within himself, and of growing forth outwardly from himself.

"Above all, therefore, it is the old within the child which clarifies, unfolds and transmutes itself, thus developing that which is new. The whole process takes place according to a definite law resting in the child himself, in his life, in life as such."—*P., p. 168.*

We have seen that Froebel draws no hard and fast line between sensation and thought. On more than one occasion, he does refer to something less definite than a perception, in one passage using the word "Eindrück," and in another the term "Vorentwickelung," translated by Miss Jarvis as "preliminary impression," of which he says it is "to be raised later, at the right time, by look and by word, to a clear perception."—*P., p. 86.*

In "The Education of Man," Froebel's earlier work, he deals with the function of language, "the word," in differentiating "the misty formless darkness," the nothing, the mist.

"At an early period there come, too, on the part of the parents, corresponding words which at first separate the child from the outer world, but afterwards re-unite them. With the help of these words, these objects present themselves, at first singly and rarely, but later in various combinations and more frequently in their self-contained definite individuality. At last man—the child—beholds himself as a definite individual object, wholly distinct from all others."—*E., p. 40.*

The function of the name, as calling attention to the thing, seemed to Froebel of so much consequence, that he says, "the name creates the thing for the child." It is in connection with the development of speech in the stage just following on infancy that he says: "Up to this stage, the inner being of man is still an unorganized undifferentiated unity. With language, organization sets in."

"This period is pre-eminently the period of the development of the faculty of speech. Therefore it was indispensable that whatever the child did should be clearly and definitely designated by the word. Every object, every thing, became such, as it were only through the word; before it had been named, although the child might have seemed to see it with the outer eyes, it had no existence for him. The name, as it were, created the thing for the child.—*E., p. 90.*

"The object of giving names is not primarily the development of the child's power of speech, but to assist his comprehension of the object, its parts and properties, by defining his sense-impressions."—*P., p. 242.*

Professor Stout also speaks of the casual naming of the object, by those around the child as "a means of fixing the attention of the child on the object when it would otherwise pass unnoticed," and he guards against the misconception that the name at the outset is a name for the child. He calls it "merely a special sound associated with a special percept in a quite casual and indefinite way."

Froebel, too, is careful when he says:

"A definite tone is to be connected with a definite perception, and the tone when heard again may recall the perception."

Though Froebel has little to say about the separate senses, and what little he has is worthless, yet on the other hand he has a great deal to say, especially in his later writings, about the child's bodily activity, and the experiences and perceptions (Erfahrung-Wahrnehmen) he gains from it. Indeed he makes so much of this, and it is so essentially a modern way of thinking that it has been given a chapter to itself.

CHAPTER V
How Consciousness is Differentiated.—The Place of Action in the Development of Perception and of Feeling

Once objects have begun to emerge, differentiated out of the formless indistinctness, comes what Froebel calls the "sucking-in stage," where the child "makes the external internal."

Here, more than anywhere perhaps, Froebel shows his genius, his originality as a student of child psychology, in that he perceived that this mental sucking-in is not merely a matter of sense organs, but that it is also a muscular performance.

Who, before Froebel, understood the importance of motor activity from the very earliest days, as a means of gaining ideas, or realized as we now begin to do, that this is the true explanation of the "endless imitation which is the child's vocation"?

In speaking of the "new-born child," it is activity or action which is again and again repeated and emphasized as the outstanding characteristic, "an activity and action devoted to working with and prevailing over the outer."

"As rest appears to be the earliest requirement of the bodily life, so movement soon appears as the demand of the soul life."—*P., p. 63.*

The baby's "feeble strength" is to be drawn into the game, where possible, "particularly that he may experience and perceive, directly through and in his own activity" (durch und in Eigenthätigkeit unmittelbar selbst erfahre und wahrnehme).—*P., p. 78.*

It is "through spontaneous activity, as well as through the mother's instinctive knowledge of his needs" that the child gains "the first impressions of the soul, as it were, the first cognitions."

Out of forty-nine Mother Songs, two only deal specifically with the senses, though all deal with action, and Froebel takes care to point out the close connection of sense and movement.

"Limbs and senses seem to have very different provinces of activity, and so they have; yet so deep-seated is their linked interchange that neither of them fails to react on the other. And no Games for the limbs have presented themselves to us, not even the 'Kicking Song' which have not also made demands upon the sense of sight."—*M., p. 168.*

"The use of the body and of the limbs is developed simultaneously and in the same proportion as the use of the senses, the order being determined by their own nature and the properties of the material world. Outer objects are near, or moving away, or fixed at a distance, and either invite rest, seizure and holding fast, or invite him who would bring them nearer to move towards them."—*E., p. 47.*

Froebel's account of the significance of the ceaseless activity of the young child anticipates to a certain extent that of Mr. Irving King, who, in his most interesting "Psychology of Child Development," deals expressly with "the functional relation of consciousness to activity." But the views of Professor Stout as expressed in his "Analytic Psychology," and with which Froebel's writing has already been compared, and those of Mr. Irving King do not appear to clash in any way.

Mr. King begins by discussing the "sort of consciousness" a young child must have, and concludes that it must from the very first be a unified consciousness, however vague, any discreteness being on the part of the object. He also states that the consciousness of a human being must differ from that of the animal entering life with many "ready-made complexes of adjustment," because "Consciousness is related not to activity, but to the growth of activity." We have just seen that Froebel too insists on a unified consciousness, that he too says that "the external world," though composed always of the same variety of objects, "comes to the child as 'an undifferentiated unity.'" Froebel is also quite sound as to the difference between the mental possibilities of the animal "whose instincts, as they are called, are at birth so definite and strong," and that of the child "born in the extreme condition of helplessness," by whom "everything external is to be overcome."[22]

Reflex and instinctive acts which the child brings into the world with him, says Mr. King, are unconscious, as are reflex and habitual activities to the adult, but "the checking of a movement must make the child more definitely conscious of it … it is no longer mere movement, but movement-stopped-by-something. As soon as movement stands out, as soon as the consciousness of it is interwoven with something that is not movement, we have the basis for indefinite advance."

Froebel says the same thing in the first of the Mother Songs, where he takes as the point of departure for all future training this movement-stopped-by-something, to which Mr. King refers as the earliest beginning of consciousness. The mother is told that when her baby "strikes out with his small arms, as he kicks with his feet," it is a challenge, to which she instinctively responds by giving him her hand or her chest, "against which he tramples with alternate feet and so measures and increases his strength." So, he reaches "that first consciousness of self, which is born of physical opposition to and connection with the external world."—*P., p. 171.*

Every one knows that Froebel laid much stress on the necessity for what is usually called "expression," which he called *Darstellung*—often translated "representation." One of his reasons for this emphasis is, however, by no means always understood, viz. that it "induces clear perception."

It is in discussing and criticizing Professor Baldwin's description of imitation as a circular process, that Mr. Irving King brings out two points of view from which we may regard imitation, that of the observer and that of the so-called imitator. Imitation, he says, is a term for the observer only, and not a term for psychology at all. Baldwin says that "real or persistent imitation is the reaction that will reproduce the stimulating impression and so tend to perpetuate itself." But as Mr. King shows in the case of the child who imitates his mother's poking of the fire, "the response of the child to the copy does not reinstate the original stimulus.… What the child gets is not a reproduced stimulus, but a new experience."

In "The Education of Man," written years before his whole attention was given to the young child, Froebel had emphasized the necessity for "representation" which "induces and implies clear perception."

"For what man tries to represent or do, that he begins to understand."—*E., p. 76.*

As we have seen that Froebel sets before himself the self-same task which Mr. King states as the business of the genetic psychologist, so it should be no surprise that he gives virtually the same answer to the question: What do the imitative activities mean to the child?

Mr. King's answer is that the child's emphasis is not on the copying of a certain act, but on the attainment of a certain experience that comes through the copying or imitating. "The child," he says, "is seldom or never imitating from his own point of view, but is always trying to sort out some of his own ill-organized experiences."

Froebel's words are:

"The child, though unconsciously, strives to make his inner life outwardly objective and thus perceptible, and so to become conscious of it, to see it mirrored in the outward phenomena. It is for this reason that the child tries to do himself whatever he sees done."—*P., p. 240.*

"If your child is to understand any action, you must let him carry it out himself, deeply rooted in this fact is his prompt and delighted imitation of whatever he finds around him."—*M., p. 16.*

"Thought must form itself in action, and action resolve and clear itself in thought."—*P., p. 42.*

Every stimulus, says Mr. King, is a suggestion to activity, and it is interesting to notice how two minds working on the same lines, though separated not only by years but by difference of language, can fall into almost the same phrases. Mr. King unconsciously uses almost Froebel's very words when he writes: *"The sight of the object tends to set the activity free."*

Froebel writes:

"As the ball stirs, moves, goes, runs and rolls, the child who is playing with it begins to feel the desire to do likewise.… The smallest child moves joyfully, springs gaily, hops up and down or beats with his arms when he sees a moving object. This is not merely delight in the movement of the object before him, but it is the working of the inner activity wakened in him by the sight of outer activity. *Through such vision the inner life has been freed."*—*P., p. 239.*

We have seen that according to Froebel the earliest consciousness is a kind of self-consciousness. Mr. Irving King says that the very beginning of consciousness is "movement-stopped-by-something," and Froebel says that when the baby kicks out or tramples with his feet and the mother responds by giving him her hand or chest to push against, the child reaches that "first consciousness of self which is born of physical opposition to and connection with the external world." Here again we come to a point in which Froebel's insight shows well in comparison with a typical modern genetic psychologist. "Many writers," says Mr. Irving King, "have tried to select out certain kinds of activity as peculiarly connected with the development of the infant's sense of self." Preyer, for instance, connects this development specially with painful sensations; Baldwin, with experience associated with people, as contrasted with experience of things. His own conclusion is that "it seems more correct to say that all the child's activities are factors of very nearly equal importance for developing the sense of self, as distinct from things and other people," and it is this view that we find in Froebel's writings. Even in "The Education of Man" we find:

"If man, in accordance with his destiny, is truly and thoroughly to know each thing of the surrounding world; if *with the aid of each thing he is truly and thoroughly to know himself.…"*—*E., p. 92.*

And among his later writings, in connection with the child's play with bricks Froebel says:

"True and early knowledge of Nature and of the outer world and *especially clear self-knowledge* come to the child by this early dismembering and reconstruction and perception of real things, though not as yet, by any means, through verbal designation of the various productions of childish activity."—*P., p. 123.*

"Self-consciousness," says Mr. King, "is essentially a relative and variable term for all of us. It stands for a process of definition, that, strictly speaking, proceeds till maturity, or even later." And Froebel, writing about how, through the mother's play with a ball, a child may gain his earliest perceptions of object, space and time, says that by the coming and going of the ball, etc.,

"there goes forth to the child the object, recognized as such by the mind and so held fast, the consciousness of the object, and so consciousness itself awakens in the child."

And without a pause he goes on:

"Self-consciousness belongs to the nature of man, and is one with it. To become conscious of itself is the first task in the life of the child, as it is the task of the whole life of man. That this task may be accomplished the child is, even from his first appearance, surrounded by a definite place and by objects: by the air blowing around all living creatures, as well as by the arousing, human, spiritual language of words…. Thus it is with the attainment of man to consciousness and the speech required and conditioned by that attainment to consciousness."—*P., p. 39.*

It is rather interesting to notice that in her translation of this passage in which Froebel declares that self-consciousness comes to a child as a result of all his surroundings, Miss Jarvis omits the word "self." She begins her paragraph with "Bewusstsein," instead of "Selbstbewusstsein" as it stands in the original. To quote Mr. King, "It is generally held that these are two distinct attitudes, that consciousness may exist without an accompanying consciousness of the self as separate from the objects, activities and persons of the rest of the world." Probably this was Miss Jarvis's own view, and she left out the word "self" as having no place or meaning in the context. It was, however, not meaningless to Froebel himself.

Mr. King continues: "The really important point is not to be able to put the finger down on some one thing that proves a developed self-consciousness, but to be able to show at every point that the process of definition is a function of the growing complexity of the child's activities." And, in "The First Action of a Child" Froebel writes:

"The nature of man as a being intended for self-consciousness, shows itself in the quite distinctive nature of the child's activity, even at the end of the so-called three months' slumber, in the totality of the first childish action. This cannot be better comprehended than by the expression 'to busy himself' (sich beschäftigen) in the impulse of the child—an impulse awakening simultaneously with his inner life—an impulse in close union with feeling and perception, to be active for the increasing development of his life: in this lies the nature of man as a being intended to grow towards and ultimately to become self-conscious."—*P., p. 22.*

Speaking of his second plaything, intended for a child six months old, he says:

"And so his play, and through his play, his surroundings—finally Nature and Universe—may become a mirror of himself and of his life. But this cannot be too early facilitated, that the child at once, from the first beginning of his self-developing feeling of life, may grow up in exchange and comparison with Nature and life, and as he impresses his life in form, and as form on things outside, so he may again perceive his life therein."—*P., p. 95.*

Froebel was bound to watch for early developments of self-consciousness, because his whole philosophy and pedagogy are based on his firm belief that while everything in the universe is an expression of the Divine, man alone is "destined" to express the God within "with self-determination." So, of the little child, he writes:

"Because the child himself begins to represent his inner being outwardly, he imputes the same activity to all about him, to the pebble and chip of wood, to the plant, the flower, and the animal. And thus there is developed in the child at this stage his own life, his life with parents and family, and particularly his life in and with Nature, as if this held life *like that which he feels within himself*."—*E., p. 54.*

As the child grows older, the mother, Froebel continues, tries to teach him to feel the complexity of his own body, "Give me your arm," "Where is your hand?" she says, and she "playfully leads him to a knowledge of the members which he cannot see," and the passage ends:

"The aim of all this is to lead the child to self-consciousness, to reflection about himself in the approaching period of boyhood. Thus, a boy ten years old, similarly guided by instinct, believing himself unobserved, soliloquized: 'I am not my arm, nor my ear; all my limbs and organs I can separate from myself, and I still remain myself; I wonder what I am; who and what is this which I call myself?'"—E., p. 56.

Nor does Froebel forget the idea of the self as the boy grows older.

Once the activities of running, jumping, etc., are familiar, the boy's play takes on a new complexion. His games are now "trials of strength," or "displays of strength."

"The boy tries to see himself in his companions, to feel himself in them, to weigh and measure himself by them, to know and find himself by their aid."—E., p. 114.

"The life of the boy has, indeed, no other purpose but that of the outer representation of his self: his life is in truth but an external representation of his inner being, of his power, particularly through plastic material. In the forms he fashions, he does not see outer forms which he is to take in and understand; he sees in them the expression of his spirit, of the activities of his own mind."—E., p. 279.

Surely it is another touch of genius that makes Froebel spring to the nascent idea of self as *the* reason for the child's craving for tales of all kinds.

"Knowledge of a thing can never be attained by comparing it with itself. Therefore the boy cannot attain any knowledge of the nature and meaning of his own life, by comparing it with itself ... everybody knows that comparisons with somewhat remote objects are more effective than those with very near objects. Only the study of the life of others can furnish such points of comparison with the life he has himself experienced.... It is the innermost desire and need of a vigorous boy to understand his own life.... This is the chief reason why boys are so fond of stories, legends and tales.... The story concerns other men, other circumstances, other times and places, yet the hearer seeks his own image, he beholds it, and no one knows that he sees it."—E., p. 305.

As Froebel shows so much insight into the paramount importance of action in the development of self-consciousness, it is not surprising to find that he recognizes also its special importance in the development of feeling.

It is probably to the late Professor James and his sparkling paradoxes that the educational world owes its grasp of the importance of expression in connection with feeling; we feel because we act, we are told, we do not run away because we are afraid, but we are afraid because we have run away. But all Froebelians had already learnt the truth at the bottom of this from Froebel's Mother Songs.

When he wrote his earliest and greatest book, "The Education of Man," Froebel was already far enough advanced to point out the necessity for at least verbal expression of feeling. He then advocated giving to young boys simple prayers or words by which they can express childish gratitude for care and protection, so that these feelings may be retained and deepened.

"It is natural that religious feelings and thoughts should spring up.... In the beginning these sentiments and feelings will only manifest themselves as an effect, a fullness without word or form, without any adequate expression of what they are, merely as something that uplifts our being and fills the soul. At this juncture, it is most beneficial, strengthening, and uplifting for the boy to receive words—a language for these sentiments and feelings—*so that they may not be stifled in themselves, vanish for lack of expression.*"—*E., p. 246.*

The same remark is made in connection with the teaching of poems and songs. When feeling is aroused by the contemplation of Nature, it must be expressed. When Spring brings "gladness," and Autumn "longing and hope," and when Winter awakens "courage and vigour," then:

"Man, too, would express the thoughts and feelings that are awakened in him and for which he cannot find words, and these should be given him.… the thoughtful teacher can easily interpret the thoughts and feelings of the boys, as well as the phases of Nature, in living fitting words.… In general, all that was said concerning the appropriation of religious expressions is true here."—*E., p. 267.*

Froebel had also noted even thus early how "the natural mother" from the very beginning cultivates feeling through expression, through gesture or action.

"Mother love seeks to awaken and to interpret the feeling of community between the child and the father, brother and sister, when she says, 'Dear Daddy!' as she caressingly passes the child's hand over the father's cheek. 'Love daddy, love little sister,' etc."—*E., p. 69.*

In the Mother's Songs, written much later and after Froebel had made careful observation of young children, he is more emphatic, and his ideas of expression are both wider and more definite. In "The Education of Man" he had said that literature exercises and tests judgment and feelings, and he had added that this should be followed up by some constructive action. But now he knows that feeling when stirred ought to express itself in actual service, just as James suggests "speaking genially to one's grandmother, or giving up one's seat in a horse car, if nothing more heroic offers."

The mother is told that at first she should help her little one to understand her care of him and his dependence on her by "the looking-glass of outer life," by letting him, for instance, watch the hen caring for her chickens, and the parent birds feeding and brooding over their young in the nest. In the rhymed motto of "The Nest" she is told:

"Already the baby likes to see pictures showing the loving care of a mother. Let him do so often, that his life experience may become clear to him."

But the longer explanation has an important addition:

"The way lies through our imaginative, tender and emotional observation of Nature and of man's life, and through the child's affectionately taking their most intimate meaning into the life of his own heart, *and expressing by representation what he thus takes in.*"—*M., p. 149.*

So, as the child begins to realize what he owes, comes the next little play, "The Flower Basket," the key-note of which is given in its motto:

"Try to let the child give outward form to what stirs his feelings, for the love even of a child dies away if not carefully fostered."—*M., p. 38.*

And the baby makes of his tiny hands a basket for flowers wherewith to celebrate the father's birthday in orthodox German fashion. In Froebel's own phrase, the "inner meaning" of the little finger play with its picture, is "to cherish thoughtfully the bond, which is invisible, yet which can be felt, whereby the life of humanity is bound together, the first opportunity for which is afforded by the life of the child and the family." What is important here is that Froebel has pointed out the way in which this bond can be strengthened, that is by expression, by giving "outward form to what stirs feeling."

This idea of service as expression of feeling comes into Froebel's description of the ideal child, "merry, happy, strong and busy," when the mother:

"Kissed upon his brow her blessing, Then, his love for her expressing, Off he starts his mother serving All he can do, she's deserving."—*M., p. 191.*

Again, in connection with childish productions, the little baskets, napkin rings, etc., that they have made, Froebel wrote:

"The use made of these little productions is very important to the civilizing and nourishing of the child's being and mind, for I consider the fact that many children receive so much and can give hardly anything to be one of the most essential causes of the frequent retrogression of childish love and sensibility."

Froebel always emphasizes the essential importance of family bonds in the development of feeling, and he not only instructs the mother to see to it that the child recognizes the family circle, but he tells her that he will realize his "kinship" by service done for the family.

"Family, family, you are more than School or Church … without you what are Altar and Church…."—*M., p. 159.*

"That many things are in a whole Soon dawns upon a childish soul. Then let the mother teach him carefully To know the circle of the family."—*M., p. 46.*

"Duties are not burdens, duty fulfilled leads to light, this is why every healthy child likes and enjoys doing duties, provided they speak to him clearly and simply, above all inexorably…. See how happy a child is feeling he has done his small duties. He already feels his kinship with you thereby. Cherish this feeling, and it will be salvation and blessing to him."—*M., p. 174.*

As the feeling of the adult is called out by the helplessness of a child, so, too:

"the child's sympathy is roused by the young creatures' necessities more than by anything else, and among these chiefly by their nakedness and softness: '… Mother, the poor little birds are so lonely, I am so sorry for the poor little things.'"—*M., p. 150.*

And in this connection too comes the warning that feeling must not be allowed to evaporate without action:

"If your child's to love and cherish Life that needs him day by day, Give him things to tend that perish If he ever stops away."—*M., p. 84.*

The child is "to feel within himself Nature's close interdependence":

"Whenever opportunity occurs, make this inner dependence of life clear, visible, impressive, tangible and perceptible to your child, even though it be in only a few of the essential links of this great chain, until you come to the last ring that holds all the rest, God's Father-love for all. The baker cannot bake if the miller brings him no flour, the miller can grind no flour if the farmer brings him no corn, the field can yield no crop if Nature does not work towards it in harmony, and Nature could not work in harmony if God had not placed in her power and material, and if His love did not guide everything to its fulfilment."—*M., p. 148.*

And again, as always, follows the need for expression of some kind. The children are not to be disturbed while they "say grace" over their doll's feast.

"It is no drawing down of the sacred into outer life; no, this is the germ which gives the outside actions of life the inner meaning and higher consecration, which life so much needs. For how is your child to cultivate innocently in himself a lively feeling for what is holy, if you will not grant that it takes form for him even in his innocent games."—*M., p. 148.*

It may be as well before leaving the subject to notice here one or two other points in connection with feeling that are touched upon by Froebel.

Though, as we have seen[23], the feeling side is always kept in closest connection with those of knowledge and action, yet the fundamental importance of the emotional side is stated quite distinctly. The child is "living, loving and perceiving," or "creating, feeling and thinking," still:

"The cultivation of boyhood rests wholly on that of childhood; therefore activity and firmness of the will rest upon activity and firmness of the feelings and of the heart. Where the latter are lacking, the former will scarcely be attainable."—*E., p. 97.*

This is put more strongly in connection with the child's imitation of the music of the bell note, the "bim-baum" or "ding-dong" sung by the mother, while she swings the ball to and fro, which according to Froebel "serves the emotional side."

"The children thus early and definitely point out that the centre, the real foundation, the starting-point of human development is the heart and the emotions, but the training to action and thought, the corporeal and mental, goes on constantly and inseparably by the side of it; and thought must form itself into action, and action resolve and clear itself in thought; but both have their roots in the emotional nature."—*P., p. 42.*

Another point Froebel makes in this connection, is that feeling alone can awaken feeling, and that those who complain of want of feeling in their children have probably themselves to blame. Want of good feeling and the prevalence among boys of egotism, unfriendliness, etc., is explained as:

"clearly due not merely to the failure of arousing at an early period, and of subsequently cultivating in the child a feeling of common sympathy, but also to the early annihilation of this feeling between parents and children."—*E., p. 122.*

The elders must show sympathy with the child's thoughts and feelings, they must not rest content with caring for his bodily welfare. If the child fails to find sympathy, for example in connection with his interest in Nature, if he "fails to find the same feelings among adults who suppress his germinating inner life" then, says Froebel:

"a double effect follows, loss of respect for the elder and a recoil of the original anticipation."—*E., p. 164.*

"Mothers and Fathers, is it not almost incredible how early the child appears to distinguish inner intellectual and loving gifts from outer bodily ones, or, rather, to be conscious of the heart and mind of the giver to feel the giving spirit? Who does not see this in the effect of a friendly glance, of a sympathizingly spoken word, of a tender care which often affords little more than sympathy and companionship?… It is a remarkable fact that the mere love for the outward person, the mere bodily care, does not satisfy him; indeed, the nobler the child is in his nature the less does he cling to the giving person. Through this consideration we have found and recognized what we sought, namely, that the respect and love—yea, the reverence—of children and youth are gained and secured to parents in proportion to what the latter are doing for the education of the mental life of the children.… If the lively appreciation of what has been done to cultivate his inner world fill the soul of a child, then will true love and gratitude towards parents, respect and veneration for age, germinate in the mind of a child."—*P., p. 111.*

We have spoken in this chapter of what is popularly called the instinct of imitation, and we have seen that Froebel makes much of what he calls the instinct or impulse of activity (Thätigkeitstrieb), or the instinct for employment (Beschäftigungstrieb).

It may be well now to consider what, considering the ideas of his day and generation, Froebel could find to say on a subject so important as the instinctive activities of human beings and of other animals, concerning which so much has now been written and which, according to Professor Dewey, Froebel regarded and rightly regarded as the foundation-stones of educational method.

CHAPTER VI
Instinct and Instincts

"The older writings on Instinct are ineffectual wastes of words," writes Professor James, "because their authors never came down to this simple and definite idea (that the nervous system is to a great extent a pre-organized bundle of reactions), but smothered everything in vague wonder at the clairvoyant and prophetic power of animals—so superior to anything in Man."[24]

Froebel was certainly not in a position to know much of the nervous system, but what he wrote about instinct cannot be classed with these older writings. For even without modern knowledge, he waxes indignant over the opinions of those who created James' "ineffectual wastes of words." Far from allowing that instinct in the lower animals is superior to anything in man, Froebel maintains that the very weakness, indefiniteness of man's instincts or impulses (Triebe) is a sign of his superiority.

"Notwithstanding the early manifestation in the human infant of the impulse to employment (Beschäftigungstriebe), much has been said from an entirely wrong point of view about man's helplessness at birth, and his slow development to independence, which necessitates for so long a period the care and help of the mother. It has even been said, that, in this respect, man's position is behind and below that of other animals. But that very point, which has been cited as evidence of man's imperfection, is a proof of his worth. For we recognize through this helplessness, that man is called to ever higher self-consciousness."—P., p. 24.

At the same time it should be pointed out that Froebel does not make the opposite mistake of supposing that man has no instincts. Since he approached psychology from the biological side, so far as it could be known to him, Froebel was bound to have faith in instinct, in race-habit, in tendencies which, because they have been of use to the race, are bedded in the nature of each individual. It is to Froebel's later writings and especially to the little paper, on "The First Action of a Child," that we must turn to see how wonderfully correct are his views on the whole question of instinct.

It may be better to give first the position of modern writers on the subject by quoting from the last chapter of Professor Lloyd Morgan's "Habit and Instinct," a clear and concise passage showing that the contrary schools of thought represented on the one hand by the Darwin and Romanes and on the other by Professors James and Wundt, can after all be resolved into a matter of definition.

"If, then, the question be asked, whether man has a large or a small endowment of instinct, the answer will depend upon the precise definition of 'instinct.' If we take congenital definiteness as characteristic of instinct, we shall agree with Darwin, that 'the fewness and the comparative simplicity of the instincts of the higher animals are remarkable as compared with those of lower animals;' and with Romanes that 'instinct plays a larger part in the psychology of many animals than it does in the psychology of man.' If, on the other hand, a broader definition of instinct be accepted, so as to include what is innate, in the sense before defined, we shall agree with Professor Wundt that human life is 'permeated through and through with instinctive action, determined in part, however, by intelligence and volition;' and shall not profoundly disagree with Professor Wm. James, who says that man possesses all the impulses that they (the lower animals) have and a great many more besides."

In Mr. McDougall's important contribution to the discussion of human instinct, he says that the view which is rapidly gaining ground is that the gradual evolution of intelligence "did not supplant and lead to the atrophy of the instincts, but controlled and modified their operation." As Mr. McDougall goes on to state his belief "that the recognition of the full scope and function of the human instincts will appear to those that come after us as the most important advance made by psychology in our time," it is important to the purpose of this book, to make clear to what extent Froebel's views on the subject approach those of modern writers.

Mr. McDougall makes a very clear distinction between specific tendencies to which he limits the word instinct, and non-specific or general tendencies. Naturally Froebel did not reach this standpoint, but he does seem to have thought out his terminology. He felt strongly as to the use of words of foreign origin, and generally uses "*Trieb*," "*Lebenstrieb*," "*Drang*" or "*Lebensdrang*," where we might use instinct. But he does occasionally use "instinct," notably in a passage quoted below "whose impulses, powers and abilities, whose instincts as they are called" (dessen Lebenstriebe Kräfte und Anlagen, dessen Instincte wie man es nennt), where he seems to be feeling about for the right expression. Other words in constant use are "*Neigung*," "*Streben*" and "*Richtung*," probably best translated by "tendency." It can be argued, however, that to the word Trieb Froebel does seem to have attached a more definite meaning, and his use of this word is certainly limited.

Professor James' account of instinct begins with the statement that "Every instinct is an impulse," a driving to action, but the use of the words "*Trieb*" and "*Drang*" makes such a pronouncement unnecessary to a German writer, and if this root idea is not implied by the noun, it generally, in Froebel's writings, makes its appearance in the verb. Thus we frequently read of "a longing which drives the child to," etc. (die Sehnsucht die das Kind treibt).

The merest glance through Froebel's writings is enough to show his belief in the existence of instinct in the human being. His references to it are constant. It is an impulse (Trieb) "which the child did not give himself, which came without his will, in later life even against his will," but which "urges to action" (drängt ihn dazu). It is a force so strong, that it "holds captive mind and body." The child is described as "driven by impulse" (des von Lebensdrang getriebenen Kindes). The boy again is "held captive by harmless, even praiseworthy, impulses" (sogar lobenswerten Triebe), or "gives himself up entirely to the impulses of his inner life" (dem Treibenden innern Leben).

In his earlier work, "The Education of Man," Froebel is first concerned with urging that the young human being, "a product of Nature," has instincts quite as trustworthy as those of any other young animal, and the following eloquent passage is very well known:

"The undisturbed working of the Divine Unity is necessarily good, and this implies that the young human being, still as it were in the process of creation, would seek as a product of Nature, though still unconsciously, yet decidedly and surely that which is in itself best: and, moreover, in a form wholly adapted to his condition, disposition, powers and means. Thus the duckling hastens to the pond, while the young chicken scratches the ground, and the young swallow catches his food upon the wing and scarcely ever touches the ground. We grant space and time to young plants and animals because we know that in accordance with the laws that live in them they will develop properly and grow well. Arbitrary interference with their growth is avoided because it is known that this would disturb their development; but the young human being is looked upon as a piece of wax, a lump of clay, which man can mould into what he pleases.... Thus, O parents, could your children, on whom you force in tender years forms and aims against their nature, thus could your children too unfold in beauty and develop in harmony."—*E., p. 7.*

It is true that to Froebel evolution is "the working of Divine Unity." But there seems to be no special reason why this should invalidate what Froebel has to say, any more than Sir Oliver Lodge should be disqualified as a scientist, because he has produced a book in which he writes: "Development means unfolding latent possibilities … growth and development are in accordance with the law of the universe … the law of the universe and the will of God are here regarded as in some sort synonymous terms."

This is exactly Froebel's position; he writes that

"Nature and man have their origin in one and the same eternal Being, and their development takes place in accordance with the same laws, only at different stages."—*E., p. 161.*

That Froebel not only recognized the presence of instinct in human beings, but that he also saw, as Professor Wundt puts it, that this is "determined in parts by intelligence and volition," he states very plainly:

"Natural instinct and good example will do much, but here, as in all human concerns, one must proceed by extension of knowledge, and by careful scrutiny, or both the one and the other may mislead or be misdirected. Experience cries aloud to us, to warn us of this danger. *Assuredly man ought not to neglect his natural instincts, still less abandon them, but he must ennoble them through his intelligence, purify them through his reason.*"—*L., p. 222.*

"In the progress of development three stages differentiate themselves and fall apart; and these stages are seen both in individual men, and in the race as a whole. They are:

(1) *Unconsciousness, the merely instinctive stage*;

(2) *Vague Feeling, the tendency upwards towards consciousness*; and

(3) *Relatively clear Conscious Intelligence.*

Everything that is acquired by a great unity, say by a family, a community, a nation, must in its beginnings be acquired by the single members of that unity; and further it will take them in one of the three grades of development, either that of mere unconsciousness, or of vague feeling, or in the third and highest grade, that of conscious intelligence, so far as it has been maintained by mankind up to the present time."—(Letter to Madame D. Lutkens, dated March, 1851.)

It is in "The First Action of a Child" that we find Froebel contrasting the instincts of the lower animals with those of man. Here curiously enough, Froebel, according to Professor Stout, is almost more correct than Professor Lloyd Morgan himself, whose statement "that animals do not perceive relations" Professor Stout regards as misleading. His correction is, "unless an artificial restriction is put on the meaning of the term *relation*, this statement would imply that animals cannot perceive the position of objects in space or their motion.... Hence we should say, not that the perception of relation is deficient in animals, but only that definite perception of relations is deficient which depends on comparison."

Now it is this very point of comparison which Froebel takes as the essential intellectual difference between the animal independent from birth thanks to fully developed instinct, and the child helpless and apparently inferior at first, yet destined for progress "self-active and free." He writes:

"The animal whose life impulses, powers and abilities, whose instincts as they are called (dessen Lebenstriebe, Kräfte und Anlagen, dessen Instincte wie man es nennt) are at once so definite and strong, that in natural conditions it never fails, indeed cannot fail to overcome every hindrance within its life's reach, the animal just on this account can never arrive at a knowledge of its powers, its qualities, its nature ... *for it lacks all points of comparison. It lacks all points of comparison, which, in the case of man proceed from the fact that the weakest output of strength meets with obstacles* which increase as the strength increases, and which will only with difficulty be conquered or overcome and annihilated.

"It is quite different in the life of man, in the beginning of which practically nothing can be accomplished without help from without. Nothing especially can be accomplished through a preponderance of inner power such, for example, as the newly hatched duckling shows on the water. Thus everything external must, by Man, with his preponderance of helplessness, be overcome as an obstacle solely through inner advancing, and outer strengthening and increasing of power through free activity of the will."—*P., p. 25.*

With this passage from "The First Action of a Child" we can compare the following from Stout's "Analytic Psychology":

"The peculiar feature in the life of animals which prevents progressive development is the existence of instincts which do for them what the human being must do for himself. Their inherited organization is such, that they perform the movements adapted to supply their needs on the mere occurrence of an appropriate external stimulus.... In man, a blind craving has to grope its way from darkness into light in order to become effective; in the animal the means of satisfaction are provided ready made by Nature at the outset."

After having stated that "Every instinct is an impulse," Professor James goes on to say that instinct depends upon the biological fact that the nervous system is "a pre-organized bundle of re-actions," and that when impulses block one another, an animal with many impulses, and whose mind is elevated enough to discriminate, "loses the instinctive demeanour and appears to live a life of hesitation and choice, an intellectual life."

Notwithstanding the very obvious fact that Froebel could know but little of the nervous system and its re-actions, it is still quite evident that his observation had led him to a clear recognition of the earlier stage, when "hesitation and choice" are impossible. The child, he says, "acts in obedience to an instinct which holds captive mind and body," he is "incredibly short-sighted in his obedience to instinct." That he also recognized the beginning of hesitation and choice is shown in his defence of the child who "in spite of abandonment to momentary impulse," may have "an intense inner desire for goodness," which, "if it could be appreciated in time," would make of him a good man (*E., p. 125*); and also in his plea for the early awakening and training "of judgment and of that reflection which avoids so many blunders and which, *in a natural way* (i.e. without training), does not come to man sufficiently early."—*E., p. 79.*

"Another source of boyish faults is in the precipitation, want of caution, indiscretion, in a word the thoughtlessness, the acting according to an impulse quite blameless, even praiseworthy, which holds captive all activity of mind and body, but whose consequences have not as yet entered into his experience, indeed it has not yet entered into his mind to define the consequences."—*E., p. 122.*

Froebel gives from real life a few well-chosen examples of what the boy so "incredibly short-sighted in his obedience to impulse" may do; telling how one deliberately aims a stone at a window "with earnest effort to hit it, yet without even saying to himself that if it does so, the window must be broken," and how he "stands rooted to the spot" when this happens. Another, a "very good-hearted boy, who dearly loved and took care of pigeons, aimed at his neighbour's pigeon on the roof, without considering that if the bullet hit it the dove must fall." No wonder that he urges the early awakening of that reflection (Nachdenken) which would avoid so much, and in this connection it must be remembered too that Froebel emphasized the indefiniteness of human instinct which makes comparison possible. It is also worth remarking that Froebel knew that it is only by noting consequences of actual deeds that reflection comes, and this he shows in one of his quaint parallels between "the history of creation and the development of all things."

"Similarly in each child there is repeated the deed which marks the beginning of moral and human emancipation, of the dawn of reason—essentially the same deed that marked the dawn of reason in the race as a whole."—*E., p. 41.*

It must have been a somewhat unorthodox view in 1826, but some pages further on Froebel speaks even more boldly of "the fall or—since the result is the same—the ascent of the mind of man from simple emotional development into the development of externally analytic and critical reason."—*E., p. 193.*

Professor James goes on to state two other principles which make for non-uniformity of instinct. The first of these is that instincts are inhibited by habits, and the second that instincts are transitory.

The physiological fact of "plasticity" in which these principles are grounded, was of course quite out of Froebel's ken. Nevertheless, the principles themselves do not escape his shrewd observation. Mr. McDougall points out that even acquired habits of thought and action, so important as springs of action in the developed human mind, are in a sense derived from and secondary to instincts. He goes on to say that "in the absence of instincts no habits could be formed," so it is interesting to find Froebel arguing that the phenomena of habit is a proof of the existence of what in the infant he calls the impulse to activity or to self-employment.

"The helplessness of the new-born human being in regard to all outer things is the opposite of his future ability—since life is a whole—to help himself through the enhancing of his will-power.... Helplessness and personal will, therefore, become the two points between which the child's life turns, and the fulcrum is free activity. Herein lies for the educator a key to phenomena of child-life which seem to contradict each other. For out of the impulse to activity (Thätigkeitstriebe) and to free self-employment, or rather out of the united three—helplessness, personal will, and self-employment—soon proceed custom and habit, often indolence and too facile yielding.

"Consideration of custom, and of the spontaneous acquiring of habit in the child, especially in regard to what causes it, and to its effect upon the child, is just as important for the educator, as is the consideration and guidance of his instinct of activity. This very phenomenon that the child so early accustoms and inures himself to something, this early phenomenon of child life, the growing together and becoming one, as it were, with his surroundings, is a proof of the existence and inner working, even thus early, of the impulse for activity or employment, even where the child appears outwardly inactive and passive: in that the child accommodates himself to outer surroundings, relations and requirements in order to provide more scope for his inner activity."—*P., p. 27.*

This proof may not be quite so clear to others as it was to Froebel, but at least the passage shows the close connection in his mind between instinct—the impulse towards activity and employment—and habit, and that he had noted the interaction between the two.

There are many references to the transitory nature of at least childish impulses.

"What delight a child takes in noticing what is smooth, woolly, hairy, sparkling, round, etc.… But if you do not cherish this and do not set it going in the right way, it becomes a lost thing; it grows rusty, and loses its power as a magnet loses its power when it is not sufficiently used. Power that is not at once used, effort that does not at once meet the right object— perishes."—*M., p. 181.*

"Now, at last, we would fain give another direction to the energies, desires and instincts (Kräfte, Neigungen und Triebe) of the child growing into boyhood; but it is too late. For the deep meaning of child-life passing into boyhood we not only failed to appreciate, but we misjudged it; we not only failed to nurse it, but we misdirected and crushed it."—*E., p. 75.*

"See parents, the first impulse to activity, the first constructive impulse (Bildungstrieb) comes from man according to the nature of the working of his mind, unconsciously, unrecognized, without his will, as man can indeed perceive in himself in later life. If, however, this inner summons to activity (diese innere Aufforderung zur Thätigkeit) meets with outer hindrance, especially such a one as the will of the parents, which cannot be set aside, the power is at once weakened in itself, and with many repetitions of this weakening, falls into inaction."— *E., p. 100.*

"The neglect of inner power causes the inner power itself to vanish."—*E., p. 133.*

"It is true there are few such children; but there would be more, were we not ignorantly blunting so many tendencies in our children, or starving them into inanition."—*E., p. 220.*

Writing of the origin of boyish faults Froebel says:

"When we look for the sources of these shortcomings … we find a double reason, first, complete neglect of the development of certain sides of human life, secondly early misdirection, early unnatural stages in development, and distortion, through arbitrary interference with human powers, qualities and tendencies good in their source.… Therefore at the bottom of every shortcoming in man, lies a crushed, frustrated quality or tendency, suppressed, misunderstood or misguided."—*E., pp. 119-121.*

When we come to the enumeration of the various human instincts we find that Froebel can hardly be said to have omitted any that are important from an educational point of view, except perhaps the instinct of fear, and to this he would be loth to appeal.[25] Moreover, it can be shown that his explanation of certain tendencies suggests a better basis of classification than is supplied by certain recent writers, who might be expected to surpass him with ease.

Before the publication of Mr. McDougall's "Social Psychology," there were but few attempts at any classification of instincts within at least the reach of English readers. In July, 1900, there appeared an article in "The Pedagogical Seminary" in which Mr. Eby proposed to reconstruct the Kindergarten on the basis of natural instinct. The writer had apparently no dawning idea that this was the original basis[26] of the institution he proposes to reform, but Froebel's account of Instinct shows in certain ways a clearer understanding of the subject than does his own.

Mr. Eby's tabulation was:

I. Language—with gesture and expression. II. Curiosity, or Instinct for Knowledge. III. Play

Instinct. (*a*) Motor Plays. (*b*) Hunting and Wandering. (*c*) Imitative. (*d*) Constructive. (*e*) Agricultural. (*f*) Improvised. IV. Artistic and Aesthetic Instincts. V. Social Instinct. VI. Instinct of Acquisition and Ownership. VII. Number Instinct. VIII. Interest in Stories.   Another classification, well known at least to teachers, is that given by Mr. Kirkpatrick in his "Fundamentals of Child Study."[27]

His list comprises:
I. Individual or Self-preserving Instincts. (Feeding, Fear and Fighting.) II. Parental Instincts. III. Social or Group Instincts. (Gregariousness, Sympathy, Love of Approbation, Altruism.) IV. Adaptive Instincts. (Imitation, Play, Curiosity.) V. Regulative. (Moral, Religious.) VI. Resultant and Miscellaneous. (Including such tendencies as those of collecting and constructing, and the tendency to adornment, with the æsthetic pleasure of contemplating beautiful objects.)

Interesting, helpful and suggestive as these lists are, they both serve as examples of the difficulty, if not impossibility, of any hard-and-fast lines of classification. For example, regulative instincts, which Mr. Kirkpatrick divides into moral and religious, must be derived from social instincts; gregarious instincts cannot be satisfactorily separated from instincts of self-preservation, and surely all instincts must be adaptive.

Froebel's account of the instincts of a child in some ways resembles that of Mr. McDougall, and it is certainly in some points more enlightening than either of the others.

Under the heading of Investigation, Froebel brings both the Number Instinct, and the Interest in Stories, to which Mr. Eby gives a position as fundamental as that of the Social Instinct. The constructive instinct which Mr. Kirkpatrick brings under "Resultant and Miscellaneous," has a very special place in Froebel's account, as being one way of imitating, that is another mode of investigating the surroundings, and also what is equally important, a way by which the child gains a knowledge of his own power, reaches Self-Consciousness.

It is because of the emphasis Froebel continually lays upon the developing self-consciousness that his views somewhat tend to resemble those of Mr. McDougall, though it would be absurd to attempt to draw any parallel. For Froebel, though he in no way minimizes the importance of Imitation, and although it is as the apostle of Play that he is most widely known, yet, like Mr. McDougall, he never speaks either of an Instinct of Play nor of Imitation, that is, he never uses for these his special word Trieb; nor has he any Instinct for Religion. Curiously enough, too, Froebel, with his constant insistence on the threefold aspect of mind, partly forestalls Mr. McDougall's view that "instinctive action is the outcome of a distinctly mental process, one which is incapable of being described in purely mechanical terms, … and one which, like every other mental process, has and can only be fully described in terms of the three aspects of all mental process, the cognitive, the affective, and the conative aspects."

It is in connection with the very earliest activity that Froebel writes:

"The first phenomenon of awakening child-life is activity. It is an inner activity, showing itself by consideration of and working with what is outer, by overcoming hindrances and subduing the outer. The nature of man as growing towards, and destined to reach self-consciousness, is shown in the quite peculiar character of childish activity even as early as when the infant awakes from its so-called three months' slumber. It is shown in the child's impulse to busy himself (in dem Triebe sich zu beschäftigen) in the instinct, *one with feeling and perception*, to be active for the progressive development of his own life.

"We are repeatedly impressed with the conviction that everything that is to be done for the specifically human development of the child must be connected with the fostering of this instinct to employ himself. For *this instinct corresponds to man's triune activity of doing, feeling and thinking. It corresponds to the essential nature of humanity, which is to have power and understanding, to become ever more and more self-conscious and self-determining."—P., p. 24.*

In the last sentence of this passage, which refers to the merest infant, and which immediately precedes Froebel's comparison of human instincts with those of the lower animals, are indicated the lines on which we may say Froebel classified though he never did so formally. He deals only with the "purely" or "specifically" human, as he never tires of reiterating, so that fundamental animal instincts, self-preserving and race-preserving, such as feeding and the sexual impulse, are little noticed, and only in connection with the necessity for self-control.

But, as with Mr. McDougall much is made to depend on self-feeling, so with Froebel still more does everything centre round that self-consciousness which to him is of the very nature of man, and which is made possible by the undefined or undeveloped character of human instinct.

The instincts and impulses noted by Froebel, all, be it clearly understood, in the service of the growing self-consciousness, and self-determination are: the instinct to independent activity (der Trieb zur Frei- und Selbst-thätigkeit), the instinct to investigation (Forschungstrieb), with which Froebel deals very thoroughly and by which he explains a great deal, the impulse of acquisition, the instinct of construction or formation (Bildungstrieb Gestaltungstrieb), the social instinct and the maternal instinct.

Froebel himself never tabulates, yet his apparently careful use of the word Trieb, taken along with his convincing explanations of various tendencies (Richtungen, Neigungen, Streben) seems to show that in relation to instinct there were in his mind two pairs of ideas, so closely related as to be inseparable, viz.:

(*a*) Investigation and Control of Surroundings, and (*b*) Consciousness of Self and Self-Determination.

It is impossible to become conscious of one's self except by becoming conscious of a world of objects.[28] It is equally impossible to become self-determining without gaining control over these objects, over the surroundings. In order to control the surroundings, one must first investigate them, and this investigation brings with it self-consciousness, knowledge of one's own powers and consequent self-determination. All this seems fully in accordance with what has been already stated as to the close connection between volitional and intellectual development.

The two main lines on which instinctive action must run, if it is to be, as it must be, adaptive, are given in Froebel's words, "to have power and understanding." To adapt ourselves to our surroundings we must first know them, and secondly, have power over them. Even this separation into firstly and secondly is more a matter of words than of reality. No one knew more clearly or emphasized more strongly than Froebel that action, by which alone we gain power, is also the child's royal road to knowledge. This he states very plainly in the "Plan" which he drew up for the school at Helba, which unfortunately never came into existence.

"The institution will be fundamental inasmuch as in training and instruction it will rest on the foundation from which proceed all genuine knowledge and all genuine practical attainments; it will rest on life itself and on creative effort, on the union and interdependence of doing and thinking, representation and knowledge, art and science. The institution will base its work on the pupil's personal efforts in work and expression, making these, again, the foundation of all genuine knowledge and culture. Joined with thoughtfulness these efforts become a direct medium of culture; joined with reasoning, they become a direct means of instruction and thus make of work a true subject of instruction."—E., p. 38.

Knowledge of his surroundings is however not the only knowledge that the child gains through action; this is his only way of gaining knowledge of himself, of his power and of his weakness. It is through outward activity that, as Froebel says, he "comes to self-consciousness and learns to order, determine and master himself," and it is in connection with the earliest Impulse to Activity that Froebel writes:

"The present effort of mankind is an effort after freer self-development, freer self-formation, freer determining of one's own destiny.... Therefore the more or less clear aim of the individual is Consciousness, the attaining of clearness about himself and about life in its unity as well as in its thousand ramifications, to attain to *comprehension and right use* of life.... That this highest aim may be accomplished, the present time lays upon the educator the indispensable obligation—to understand the earliest activity, the first action of the child, the impulse (Trieb) to spontaneous activity, which appears so early; to foster the impulse (Trieb) for self-culture and self-instruction, through independent doing, observing and experimenting."—*P., p. 15.*

"The first spontaneous employments of the child are noticing his environment, and play, that is, independent outward action, living outside himself.... The deepest foundation of all the phenomena, of the earliest activity of the child is this; that he must exercise the dim anticipation of conscious life, and consequently must exercise power, test and thus compare power, exercise independence, test and thus compare the degree of independence."—*P., pp. 29-31.*

"All outer activity of the child has its distinctive and ultimate ground in his inmost nature and life. The deepest craving of this inner life, this inner activity, is to behold itself mirrored in some external object. In and through such reflection the child learns to know his own activity, its essence, direction and aim, and learns also to order and determine his activity in correspondence with the outer phenomena. Such mirroring of the inner life, such making of the inner life objective is essential, for through it the child comes to self-consciousness, and learns to order, determine and master himself. The child must perceive and grasp his own life in an objective manifestation before he can perceive and grasp it in himself."—*P., p. 238.*

It may seem very presumptuous to venture to discuss here the classification of instincts adopted by Mr. McDougall, yet there are in it a few points which would not have appealed to Froebel, and it is conceivable that Mr. McDougall might make alterations in a future edition and attach even more importance to positive self-feeling as Froebel would undoubtedly have done. It is impossible to imagine Froebel having any dealings with an Instinct of Self-Abasement, though the Instinct of Self-Assertion is in full accordance with his ideas. And while it is hard to see the biological utility of an Instinct of Self-Abasement, it does seem as if the frustration of the Instinct of Self-Assertion might be made to cover all that is brought under its opposite.

It is difficult, too, to imagine Froebel allowing an Instinct of Pugnacity, and Mr. McDougall allows that this presupposes the other instincts, and that it cannot strictly be brought under his own definition of instinct. He allows, too, that this instinct is "lacking in the constitution of the females of some species," and it seems impossible not to notice the difference between little boys and girls in this respect. Surely it puts too much to the credit of mere pugnacity to say: "A man devoid of the pugnacious instinct would not only be incapable of anger, but would lack this great source of reserve energy, which is called into play in most of us by any difficulty in our path."[29] The Instinct of Self-Assertion, if it is worth anything, ought to be sufficient not only to produce anger,[30] but also to call up reserve energy to deal with difficulties. Certainly Froebel would have said so. No doubt it is because of her weaker physique that the woman has not the pugnacity of the man, but Froebel too wrote mainly of the boy, and he puts boyish tussling and fighting down to the instinctive desire to measure and to increase power and this can easily be matched on the female side, though the power measured may not be that of muscle.

"At this age the healthy boy brought up simply and naturally never evades an obstacle, a difficulty; nay he seeks it and overcomes it. 'Let it lie,' the vigorous youngster exclaims to his father, who is about to roll a piece of wood out of the boy's way—'let it lie, I can get over it.' With difficulty, indeed, the boy gets over it the first time; but he has accomplished the feat by his own strength. Strength and courage have grown in him. He returns, gets over the obstacle a second time, and soon he learns to clear it easily.… The most difficult thing seems easy, the most daring thing seems without danger to him, for his prompting comes from the innermost, from his heart and will."—*E., p. 102.*

"Many of the plays and occupations of boys at this age are predominantly mere practice and trials of strength, and many aim simply at display of strength.… *The boy tries to see himself in his companions, to feel himself in them, to weigh and measure himself by them, to know and find himself with their help.*"—*E., pp. 112-114.*

In passing, it may be suggested that it hardly seems worth while to postulate an Instinct of Repulsion with the impulses or actions of rejecting evil-tasting substances from the mouth and of shrinking from objects which are slimy or slippery. Surely the rejection of unsuitable food might be a compound reflex action tending to the preservation of health; while shrinking from slimy objects, and even from the touch of fur, might have had their uses in the case of children left in caves, and might be drawn under the instinct of fear.

There does not seem to be anything to which Mr. McDougall would take exception in what Froebel has to say about Play or about Imitation.

As to play, Froebel must be regarded as a pioneer in the attempt to explain a subject all important to educators, and by his explanation certain kinds, and notably imitative play find an appropriate place under his instinct of investigation (Forschungstrieb).

"The means of shadowing forth to the child his own nature and that of the cosmos are his play and playthings."—*P., p. 201.*

As the word Investigation certainly implies activity, it may be permissible to wonder why Mr. McDougall has not made use of the terms "The Instinct of Investigation and the Emotion of Curiosity," the more so that he himself has clearly a strong inclination to use the word curiosity to express emotion.[31]

Imitation, as we have seen,[32] is, according to Froebel, action which renders a child conscious of what is around him, conscious of his inner life of perceptions, ideas and feelings, conscious of his own power. Froebel also points out that imitation, as well as habit, is the outcome of a more fundamental impulse to activity.

"It is just as important to notice the habits of a child, especially with regard to cause and effect, as it is to notice and to foster its impulse to activity.… As now habit springs from free and spontaneous activity, so too does imitation, and it is no less important for the fostering of child-life to keep in view this origin of imitation, than it is to keep in view the phenomena of habit, custom and independent activity. For we see the whole inner life of the child manifest itself as a tri-unity in the threefold phenomenon of spontaneous activity, habit and imitation. These three phenomena are closely united in early childhood, and give us most important discoveries concerning child-life, as to foundation and result and surest guides for the early correct treatment of the child."—*P., p. 27.*

Mr. McDougall notes "at least three distinct classes" of imitative actions. The first class consists of expressive actions, secondary to the sympathetic induction of the emotions they express, as when a child responds to a smile with a smile, and here we remember how Froebel notes the child's first smile to his mother as the earliest sign of what he calls "the feeling of community." The third class is the deliberate and voluntary imitation of an admired person, which does not concern us here. The second class are "simple ideo-motor actions evoked by the visual presentation of a movement," and as a parallel to this we have Froebel's "working of the inner activity wakened by the sight of outer activity."

"The smallest child moves joyfully, springs gaily, hops up and down, or beats with his arms when he sees a moving object. This is certainly not merely delight in the movement of the object before him, but *it is the working of inner activity wakened in him by the sight of outer activity*. Through such vision the inner life has been freed...."—*P., pp. 239-40.*

A point to which exception may well be taken is that in the infant Froebel notes what he seems to regard as a fundamental tendency, the impulse or instinct of activity, or as he frequently puts it, the impulse to busy oneself, which, however, soon differentiates into two more specific tendencies, viz. the impulse to investigate and the constructive impulse.

"What formerly the child did only for the sake of activity, the boy now does for the sake of the result or product of his activity. The child's impulse to activity (Thätigkeitstrieb) has in the boy become a constructive, a formative impulse (Bildungs-Gestaltungstriebe), in which the whole outer life of the boy finds at this stage its outlet."—*E., p. 99.*

It may be worth mentioning that Groos would like to assume a "universal impulse to activity," and though he "can only hold fast to the primal need for activity," yet according to him Ribot approaches this assumption.—("The Play of Man," *p. 3*).

Even in the infant, however, this instinct or impulse to activity is devoted to "penetrating what is outer," and the Kindergarten, meant for children from three to six, is intended to foster the three instincts, activity, investigation and construction, as well as to cultivate the social instinct by placing a little child among his equals. Froebel describes it in his plan as:

"An Institution for fostering of family life and for shaping the life of the nation and human life generally, through cultivating the human instincts of activity, of investigation (Forschungstrieb), and of construction in the child, as a member of the family, of the nation, and of humanity...."—*P., p. 6.*

As regards the child, the word Trieb, which is exactly equal to impulse, seems to be applied only in one other direction, to what we would call the social instinct, and here again Froebel shows his recognition of the vagueness and indefiniteness of early consciousness. As he attributes to the infant the one impulse to activity which differentiates later into Investigation and Construction, so in the infant he recognizes a "feeling of community" (Gesammtgefühl), but says that it differentiates later into something more definite.[33]

"The development of man constitutes an unbroken whole, steadily and continuously progressing, gradually ascending. The feeling of community (Gemeingefühl) awakened in the infant, develops in the child into impulse, inclination (entwickelt sich in dem Kinde der Trieb, die Neigung)."—*E., p. 95.*

Under the important Instinct of Investigation, or the Instinct for Self-Instruction, Froebel includes a great deal. Many different activities until recently somewhat carelessly talked of collectively as "play," Froebel has separated and explained as the child's way of investigating his surroundings. Even "the earliest activity and first action of the child," Froebel says, shows "the instinct to self-teaching and self-instruction."

Imitative action or imitative play is always referred to as action which helps towards understanding of the surroundings. In the "Mother Songs" we read:

"Your child will certainly understand all the better if you make him take a part—though it be only by imitation—in what grown-up people are doing in their anxiety to maintain life. …"—*M., p. 141.*

"I have already said that this little game arose because people felt that a child's love of activity, and his striving to get the use of his limbs, ought to be carried on in such a way as to lift him at once into the complexity of the life which surrounds him.… Pray do not disturb them in their ingenious charming play (saying grace over the dolls' feast), but rather avoid noticing it if you cannot identify yourself with its charm.… For how is your child to cultivate in himself the feeling of what is holy, if you will not grant that it takes form for him in all its purity in his innocent games."—*M., p. 148.*

"What man tries to represent he begins to understand."—*E., p. 76.*

Representation, however, may be carried out in many ways, by the use of material, as well as by bodily action so that the constructive instinct also subserves that of investigation.

"To grasp a thing through life and action is much more developing, cultivating and strengthening than merely to receive it through the verbal communication of ideas. Similarly, representation of a thing by material means, in life and action, united with thought and speech, is more developing than merely verbal representation of ideas."—*E., p. 279.*

"The child must perceive and grasp his own life in an objective manifestation before he can perceive and grasp it in himself. This law of development, prescribed by Nature and by the essential character of the child, must always be respected and obeyed by the true educator. Its recognition is the aim of my gifts and games apprehended relatively to the educator."—*P., p. 38.*

Here Froebel has plainly stated the main object of his specially selected play-material. The ordinary parent not being "the man advanced in insight," who "makes clear to himself the purpose of playthings," Froebel often saw children supplied with expensive but unsuitable toys, toys which would not bring the child any nearer his destination, "to have power and understanding, to become ever more and more self-conscious and self-determining."

"Here, then, we meet as a great imperfection in ordinary playthings, a disturbing element which slumbers like a viper under roses, viz. that it is too complex, too much finished. The child can begin no new thing with it, cannot produce enough variety by it; his power of creative imagination, his power of giving outward form to his own idea is thus actually deadened. When we provide children with too finished playthings, we deprive them of the incentive to perceive the particular in the general (*P., p. 122*).… What presents are most prized by the child? Those which afford him a means of unfolding his inner life most freely and of shaping it in various directions."—*P., p. 142.*

"The man, advanced in insight, should be as clear as possible in his own mind about all this before he introduces his child into the outer world. Even when he gives the child a plaything, he must make clear to himself its purpose, and the purpose of playthings and occupation material in general. This purpose is, to aid the child freely to express what is in him and to bring the phenomena of the outer world nearer to him."—*P., p. 171.*

"To realize his aims, man, and more particularly the child, requires material, if it be only a bit of wood or a pebble with which he makes something or which he makes into something. In order to lead the child to the handling of material, we gave him the soft ball, the wooden sphere and cube, etc., discussed in the chapters on the Kindergarten Gifts. Each of these gifts incites the child to free spontaneous activity, to independent movement."[34]—*P., p. 237.*

As the child grows older his constructions advance, but still they connect themselves with investigating:

"Here he makes a little garden under the hedge; there he represents the course of the river in his furrow and in his ditch; there he studies the effects of the fall or pressure of water upon his little water-wheel."—*E., p. 105.*

Investigating naturally leads to exploring, "external objects invite him who would bring them nearer to move toward them," and so the child once he is able to stand begins to travel:

"When the child makes his first attempts at walking he frequently tries to go to some particular object. This effort may have its source in the child's desire to hold himself firm and upright by it, but we also observe that it gives him pleasure to be near the object, to touch it, to feel it, and perhaps also—a new phase of activity—to be able to move it. Hence we see the child hops up and down before it and beats on it with his little hands, in order to assure himself of the reality of the object, and to notice its qualities.… Each new phenomenon is a discovery in the child's small and yet rich world—e.g. one can go round the chair, one can stand before, behind, beside it, but one cannot go behind the bench or the wall. He likes to change his relationship to different objects, and through these changes he seeks self-recognition and self-comprehension, as well as recognition of the different objects which surround him, and recognition of his environment as a whole. Each little walk is a tour of discovery; each object is an America—a new world, which he either goes around to see if it be an island, or whose coast he follows to discover if it be a continent."—*P., p. 243.*

The boy has lost none of this tendency to explore, but he goes further afield, and it is worth noting that because the boy has a distinct purpose in view his exploring is distinctly called work.

"If activity brought joy to the child, work now gives delight to the boy. Hence the daring and venturesome feats of boyhood; the explorations of caves and ravines; the climbing of trees and mountains; the searching of heights and depths; the roaming through fields and forests.… To climb a new tree means to the boy the discovery of a new world.… Not less significant of development is the boy's inclination (Neigung) to descend into caves and ravines, to ramble in the shady grove and dark forest."—*E., pp. 102-5.*

Even the baby shows trace of the collecting or acquiring instinct, but to Froebel this still falls under the head of investigation. The child who has just learned to walk is:

"attracted by the bright round smooth pebble, by the quaint brilliant leaf, by the smooth piece of wood, and he tries to get hold of these with the help of the newly acquired use of his limbs. Look at the child that can scarcely keep himself erect and that can walk only with the greatest care—he sees a twig, a bit of straw; painfully he secures it.… See the child laboriously stooping and slowly going forward under the eaves. The force of the rain has washed out of the sand small, smooth, bright pebbles, and the ever-observing child gathers them."—*E., p. 72.*

The boy, still only from six to eight years old, keeps up the collecting habit with more method and with a wider range, and he demands assistance.

"Not less full of significance, nor less developing, is the boy's inclination to descend into caves and ravines, to ramble in the shady grove and in the dark forest. It is *the effort (Streben)* to seek and find the new, to see and discover the hidden, the desire to bring to light and *to appropriate* that which lies concealed in darkness and shadow.

"From these rambles the boy returns with rich treasures of unknown stones and plants, of animals—worms, beetles, spiders and lizards, that dwell in darkness and concealment. 'What is this? What is its name?' etc., are the questions to be answered; and every new word enriches his world and throws light upon his surroundings. Beware of greeting him with the exclamation, 'Fie, throw that down, that is horrid!' or 'Drop that, it will bite you!' If the child obeys, he drops and throws away a considerable portion of his power."—E., p. 104.

This quotation brings us to another mode of investigation, that of asking questions, which Froebel was not likely to miss.

"The child, your child, ye fathers, follows you wherever you go. Do not harshly repel him. Show no impatience about his ever-recurring questions. Every harshly repelling word crushes a bud of his tree of life.… Question upon question comes from the lips of the boy thirsting for knowledge—How? Why? When? What for? and every satisfactory answer opens to him a new world."—E., p. 86.

Professor O'Shea has an interesting section on what he calls "The Sense of Location," which he says is "at the bottom of one of the most interesting and important phenomena of adjustment—the questioning activity." So it may be worth while to notice that Froebel, whom the Professor has dismissed with one slighting reference, has been beforehand with him here, and has dealt with this same early beginning in one of his earliest Mother Songs, viz. "It's all Gone," where he says to the mother:

"How can the child understand that anything is "all gone," yet he must see sense in it or he will not be satisfied. What he saw just now is there no longer, what was above is below, what was there has vanished."—M., p. 18.

Questioning implies language, but Froebel has no language instinct. He does, however, call speech immediate (unmittelbar), usually translated "innate," and he does say that because others talk to him, the child's capacity for speech will develop of necessity and will break forth spontaneously.

It is in connection with the child's earliest investigations that Froebel brings in the learning to speak. In "The Education of Man," he notes how the young child brings all his discoveries, "his treasures," to the mother's lap, and she is warned to give the right kind of help and at the right time.

"It is the longing for interpretation that urges the child to appeal to us, it is the intense desire for this that urges him to bring his treasures to us and to lay them in our laps. The child loves all things that enter his small horizon and extend his little world. To him the least thing is a new discovery; but it must not come dead into the little world, nor lie dead therein lest it obscure the small horizon and crush the little world."—E., p. 73.

All the help the mother need give at first is to supply names, since as Froebel says, "the name, as it were, creates the thing for the child." Later she must help him to compare and classify.

"How little is needed from those around the child to aid him in this tendency (to seek for knowledge). It is only necessary to name, to put into words what the child does, sees and finds."—E., p. 75.

"It is as well while the child is making these first experiments (at walking about the room) to name the objects—e.g. There is the chair, the table, etc.… The object of giving these names is not primarily the development of the child's power of speech, but to assist his comprehension of the object, its parts and its properties by defining his sense-impressions. By a rich store of such experiences the capacity for speech develops of necessity, and speech breaks forth of itself, as it were, through heightened mental self-activity in accordance with the nature of mind."—*P., p. 242.*

Expression, of course, of which speech is but one form, is to Froebel all-important. "Speech," he says, is "required and conditioned by the attainment to consciousness," and as self-consciousness is the characteristic of humanity, so speech is "the first manifestation of mankind." In his "Autobiography" Froebel writes:

"Mankind as a whole, as one great unity, had now become my quickening thought. I kept this conception continually before my mind. I sought after proofs of it in my little world within and in the great world without me; I desired by many a struggle to win it, and then to set it worthily forth. And thus I was led back to the first appearance of man upon our earth, and to the first manifestation of mankind, his speech."—*A., p. 84.*

In talking of the mother's play with an infant he says that she accompanies every action with words, "even if obliged to confess that there can be no understanding of the spoken word," as "the general sense of hearing is not yet developed, still less the special sense of hearing words." Froebel says she is right:

"for that which will one day develop and which must originate, begins and must begin when there is as yet only the conditions, the possibility thereof. Thus it is with the attainment of the human being to consciousness, and the speech required and conditioned by consciousness."—*P., p. 40.*

Words, says Froebel, first separate the child from the world outside him.

"Up to this stage (the beginning of speech), the inner being of man is still an unmembered, undifferentiated unity. With language, the expression and representation of the internal begin; with language, organization, or a differentiation with reference to ends and means sets in."—*E., p. 50.*

Both in the earlier "Education of Man," and in his later writings Froebel uses the strong expression that "the word creates the thing" for the child, and in one passage he adds that by language the idea is defined and retained.

"This period is pre-eminently the period of the development of speech. Therefore in all the child did, it was indispensable that what he did should be clearly designated by words. Every object, every thing became such, as it were, only through the word; before it had been named although the child might have seemed to see it with the outer eyes, it had no existence for the child. The name, as it were, created the thing for the child; hence the name and the thing seemed to be one."—*E., p. 90.*

"Through her little rhymes the mother will make clear to the little one what he has done, and so his accidental productions will become a point of departure for his self-development. Word and form are opposite and yet related. Hence the word should accompany the form as its shadow. In a certain sense, giving a form a name really creates the form itself. Through the name, moreover, the form is retained in memory and defined in thought."—*P., p. 192.*

Of very early speech Froebel says that it shows:

"the peculiarity and requirement of the human mind to render itself intelligible to clarify itself by communication with others."—*P., p. 56.*

Having investigated his surroundings, near or far, and collected what seems to him attractive, the child, whether older or younger, arranges his treasures in some way, and this arrangement implies some comparison. "Like things must be ranged together and things unlike must be separated," says Froebel of the child "scarce able to walk," who has collected "the small, smooth, pebbles washed out of the sand by the rain." This "arranging objects of each kind singly in a row" is at first no doubt only a recognition of the like and unlike, but Froebel notes that it is also one way in which the child may arrive at "the capacity for counting" by which his sphere of knowledge is again extended.

"The knowledge of the relations of quantity adds much to a child's life.… At first he places together similar objects.… Who has not had frequent opportunity to observe how the child arranges the objects of each kind singly in a row. Let the mother supply the quickening word, saying Apple, apple, apple, etc. All apples. Pear, pear, pear, etc. All pears.… One pear, another apple, another apple.… Instead of the indefinite word "another" the mother subsequently uses the numerals, counting together with the child, thus: One apple, two apples, three apples, etc."— *E., p. 80.*

To many children, however, counting may come through efforts to draw. I have seen a child of four-and-a-half, in drawing a man, make a line for the arm, then lay down her pencil to count her own fingers and then draw five lines for the man's hand. Froebel says:

"The representation of objects by drawing, and the exact perception conditioned and required by the representation, soon leads the child quickly to recognize the constantly repeated association of certain numbers of different objects—e.g. two eyes and two arms, five fingers, etc. Thus the drawing of the object leads to the discovery of number.… By the development of the capacity for counting, the child's sphere of knowledge, his world, is again extended.… He was unable to determine relative quantities, but now he knows that he has two large and three small pebbles, four white and five yellow flowers," etc.—*E., p. 80.*

Yet another mode of Investigation is that of Experimenting; every normal child is what Froebel calls "a self-teaching scientist."

"The material must be known not only by its name, but by its qualities and uses.… For this reason the child examines the object on all sides; for this reason he tears and breaks it; for this reason he puts it in his mouth and bites it. We reprove the child for his naughtiness and foolishness; and yet he is wiser than we who reprove him. An instinct which the child did not give himself, the instinct which rightly understood and rightly guided would lead him to know God in his works, drives him to this."—*E., p. 73.*

It may well be through his ceaseless experimenting that the little child begins to draw, gains what the late Mr. Ebenezer Cooke called "a language of line," or as Froebel puts it, notices "linear phenomena, which direct his attention to the linear properties of surrounding objects."

"A child has found a pebble, a fragment of lime or chalk. In order to determine by experiment its properties, he has rubbed it on a board near by, and has discovered its property of imparting colour. See how he delights in the newly discovered property, how busily he makes use of it! … but soon he begins to find pleasure in the winding, straight, curved, and other forms that appear. These linear phenomena direct his attention to the linear properties of surrounding objects. Now the head becomes a circle, and now the circular line represents the head, the elliptical curve connected with it represents the body; arms and legs appear as straight or broken lines, and these again represent arms and legs; the fingers he sees as straight lines meeting in a common point, and lines so connected are, for the busy child, again hands and fingers; the eyes he sees as dots, and these again represent eyes; and thus a new world opens within and without. For what man tries to represent, that he begins to understand."—*E., p. 75.*

I have watched a child go through the process of discovering "linear phenomena," just as Froebel describes it, no doubt from his own observation. A boy of three, having folded a piece of paper for the roof of a house, was colouring it, by rubbing on red chalk, when he called out, "Oh!

I'm making lines." The other children went on rubbing, but Phil made "lines" till the roof was finished.

But Froebel does not leave unnoticed the fact that the very earliest "drawing" is an outgrowth of the muscular action to which his instinct of activity is urged by the stimulus of contact.

"Would you know how to lead the child in this matter? Watch him, he will teach you what to do. See! he is tracing the table by passing his fingers along its edges and outlines as far as he can reach, he is sketching the object on itself. This is the first and the safest step by which he becomes aware of the outlines and forms of objects. In this way he sketches and so studies the chair, the bench, the window. But soon he advances. He draws lines across the four-cornered bit of board, across the leaf of the table, or the seat of the chair, in the dim anticipation that so he can retain the forms and relations of the surfaces. Now, already he draws the form diminished.

"See! there the child has drawn table, chair and bench on a leaf of the table. Do you not see how he spontaneously trained himself for this? Objects which he could move, which were in sight, he laid on the board, and drew their form on the plane surface, following the boundaries of the objects with his hands. Soon scissors and boxes, and later leaves and twigs, even his own hand and the shadows of objects will thus be copied.

"Much is developed in the child by this action, more than it is possible to express—a clear comprehension of form, the possibility of representing the form separate from the object, the possibility of retaining the form as such, and the strengthening and fitting of hand and arm for the free representation of form."—*E., p. 77.*

Here, perhaps, is the right place to introduce what Froebel had to say about the artistic tendencies of children, since Art, to him, is always expression.

"Absolutely nothing can appear, nothing visible and sensible can come forth, that does not hold within itself the living spirit; that does not bear upon its surface the imprint of the living spirit of the being by whom it has been produced, and to whom it owes its existence. And this is true of the work of every human being—from the highest artist to the meanest labourer—as well as of the works of God, which are Nature, the creation, and all created things."—*E., p. 153.*

So, when Froebel comes to speak of art as a subject of the school curriculum he says: "Here, art will be considered only as the pure representation of the inner ... differentiated according to the material it uses, whether motion, as such, audible in sound, or visible in lines, surfaces and colours, or massive"; and he adds:

"We noticed that even at an earlier stage children have the desire to draw, but the desire also to express ideas by modelling and colouring is frequently found at this earlier stage of childhood, certainly at the very beginning of the stage of boyhood (from six years old). *This proves that art and appreciation of art constitute a general capacity or talent of man,* and should be cared for early, at latest in boyhood.

"This does not imply that the boy is to devote himself chiefly to art, and is to become an artist; but that he should be enabled to understand and appreciate true works of art. At the same time, a true education will guard him from the error of claiming to be an artist unless there is in him the true artistic calling."—*E., p. 227.*

In connection with the mother's instinctive rhythmic crooning and dandling of the infant, Froebel says:

"Thus the genuine natural mother cautiously follows in all directions the slowly developing all-sided life of the child. Others suppose him to be empty.... Thus those means of cultivation that lead so simply and naturally to the development of rhythm are lost.... Nevertheless an early development of rhythmic movement would prove most wholesome.... Even very small children, in moments of quiet, and particularly when going to sleep, will hum little strains of songs they have heard; and this should be heeded and developed as the first germ of future growth in melody and song. Undoubtedly this would soon lead in children to a spontaneity such as is shown by children in the use of speech."—*E., p. 71.*

In the "Mother Songs," too, Froebel writes:

"Hence it is so very important to rouse at least the germs of all this (the perceiving of harmony in sound and form and colour) early in a human being. If they do not develop and take shape as independent formations in life, they at least teach how to understand and recognize those of other people. This is life-gain enough. It makes a person's life richer—richer by the lives of others. And how could our earthly life be long enough to form our being with equal perfection on all sides. We can only do it by knowing and respectfully recognizing in the mirror of the lives of others what we should like to carry out ourselves. And this is as it should be, for it is by means of knowledge, regard for and respectful recognition of others, that the whole of humanity ought to represent the whole of a God-like harmonious human being."—*M., p. 162.*

In what he says of the Interest in Stories, Froebel again seems to show deeper insight than either Mr. Eby or Professor Kirkpatrick. Mr. McDougall does not touch upon the subject. It is still the outcome of the child's instinctive desire to understand himself and his surroundings. Froebel says very truly that he can only understand others in proportion as he understands himself, and can only learn to understand himself, his own life, by comparing it with that of others. The desire for stories is "a striving, a longing, a demand of the mind" (ein Streben, eine Sehnsucht, eine Forderung des Gemüthes). For the little one, the simplest story of the mother bird feeding her young ones is a help to the understanding of his own life, makes his own life objective; the mother's "effective story will hold up a looking-glass to the child, especially if it be told at the right time." For the boy the story does the same and also answers to his instinctive demand not only to understand the present, but the past:

"It is the innermost desire and need of a vigorous, genuine boy to understand his own life, to get a knowledge of its nature, its origin and outcome. Only the study of the life of others can furnish such points of comparison with the life he himself has experienced. In these the boy, endowed with an active life of his own, can view the latter as in a mirror and learn to appreciate its value. This is the chief reason why boys are so fond of stories, legends and tales; the more so when these are told as having actually occurred at some time, or as lying within the reach of probability, for which, however, there are scarcely any limits for a boy."—*E., p. 305.*

"The existence of the present teaches him the existence of the past. That, which was before he was, he would know; he would know the reason, the past cause of what now is. Who fails to remember the keen desire that filled his heart when he beheld old walls, and towers, ruins, monuments and columns on hill and the roadside—to hear others give accounts of these things, their times and causes ... thus is developed the desire and craving for tales, legends, for all kinds of stories, and later for historical accounts."—*E., p. 115.*

Even the fairy story seems to have found its legitimate place under the same heading, the instinct for investigation. Froebel sees that it covers for the little child the ground occupied by myth in the primitive consciousness. It explains the otherwise inexplicable.

"Even the present in which the boy lives still contains much that at this period of development he cannot interpret, and yet would like to interpret; much that seems to him dumb, and which he would fain have speak; ... and thus there is developed in him the intense desire for fables and fairy tales which impart language and reason to speechless things—the one within, the other beyond the limits of human relations. Surely all must have noticed this if they have given more than superficial attention to the life of boys at this age. Similarly, they must have noticed that if the boy's desire is not gratified by those around him, he will spontaneously hit upon the invention and presentation of fairy tales, and either work them out in his own mind or entertain his companions with them. These fairy tales and stories will then very clearly reveal to the observer what is going on in the innermost mind of the boy, though doubtless the latter may not himself be conscious of it."—*E., p. 116.*

"The child, like the man, would like to learn the significance of what happens around him. This is the foundation of the Greek choruses, especially in tragedy. This, too, is the foundation of very many productions in the realms of legends and fairy tales, and is indeed the cause of many phenomena in actual history. This is the result of the deeply-rooted consciousness, the deeply slumbering premonition of being surrounded by that which is higher and more conscious than ourselves."—*P., p. 146.*

The outcome of the instinct of construction, which is also so closely connected with the instinct of investigation, is that "sense of power" which *is* self-consciousness. Without this there can be no self-determination, but, says Froebel, "the sense of power must precede its cultivation." With this growing personality, too, Froebel connects what is called the instinct of Acquisition, which begins when the little child "painfully secures his bit of straw," and the boy of six to eight shows "the tendency to appropriate what he finds in the darkness of cave and forest."

"The same tendency that urges the boy to seek knowledge on the mountain and in the valley, attracts and holds him to the plain. Here he makes a garden, there he represents the course of the river, and studies the effect of the presence of water … here he has dammed up the water to form a pool.… He is particularly fond of busying himself with clear running water and with plastic materials. In these the boy who seeks self-knowledge beholds his soul as in a mirror. These employments are to him an element of his life, for now, because of a previously acquired sense of power he seeks to control and master new material. Everything must submit to his constructive instinct; there in that heap of earth he digs a cellar and on it he places a garden and a bench. Boards, branches and poles must be made into a hut, the deep, fresh snow must be rolled up to form the walls and ramparts of a fort, and the rough stones on the hill are heaped together to form a castle.… And thus each one soon forms for himself his own world; for the feeling of his own power requires and conditions also the possession of his own space and his own material belonging exclusively to him. Whether his kingdom, his province, his estate, as it were, be a corner of the yard, or of the house, or whether it be the space of a box, the human being must have at this stage an external point to which he refers all his activities, and this is best chosen and provided by himself."—*E., p. 106.*

And here, just when he is emphasizing the fast developing consciousness of self, with its demand for its own space and its own material, Froebel brings out the strength of the social instinct in boyhood. It is here that he points out that this effort to construct has a uniting, not a separating, tendency. Continuous with the last quotation comes:

"When the space to be filled is extensive, when the province to be ruled is large, when the whole to be represented is composed of many parts, then brotherly union of those who are of one mind is displayed. And when those who are of one mind meet and put their hearts into the same effort, then either the work already begun is extended or begun again as a joint production."—*E., p. 107.*

Froebel describes such joint work first in the Keilhau schoolroom—his own phrase is "education room"—where the younger boys are using building blocks, sand, sawdust, and moss, which they have brought in from the forest around and then among the older boys.

"Down yonder by the brook, how busy are the older boys with their work! They have made canals with locks, bridges and seaports, dams and mills, each undisturbed by the others. But now the water is to be used to carry ships from one level to another, and now, at every stage, each boy asserts his own rights while recognizing the rights of others. How can they settle their difficulties? Only by making agreements, and so, like States, they bind themselves by strict treaties."—*E., p. 111.*

Of games of physical movement, running, wrestling, etc., Froebel writes:

"It is the sense of power, the sense of its increase, both as an individual and as a member of a group, that fills the boy with joy, in these games.… The boy tries to see himself in his companions, to weigh and measure himself by them, to find and know himself by their help. Thus the games directly influence and educate the boy for life, they awake and cultivate many civic and moral virtues. Every town should have its common playground for the boys. Glorious would be the results from this for the entire community. For at this stage of development games whenever possible are held in common, thus developing the sense of community and the laws and requirements of a community."—*E., p. 113.*

Froebel had studied boys to some purpose, and he tells us not, however, to expect too much in the way of social virtues. Justice, self-control, honesty, courage and "severe criticism of pleasant indolence" may be expected, but mutual forbearance and consideration for those who are weaker or less familiar with the game, though not entirely lacking, are referred to as "the more delicate blossoms" of the playground. It is here that he says with wise moderation, "The feeling of power must precede its cultivation."

The social instinct does not suddenly spring into existence in boyhood. It has its roots in what Froebel calls the Feeling of Community which unites the child first with the mother, then with father, brothers and sisters.

"We cannot deny that there is at present among children and boys little gentleness, mutual forbearance … indeed, there is much egotism, unfriendliness and roughness. This is clearly due not only to the absence of early cultivation of the feeling of community, but this sympathy between parents and children is too often disturbed, yes even annihilated."—*E., p. 119.*

The sympathy of the little child ought to be trained and is trained by the wise mother always through action.

"Mother love seeks to awaken and to interpret the feeling of community, which is so important, between the child and the father, brother and sister, saying while she draws the child's little hand caressingly across the face of the father or of the little sister, 'Love the dear father—the little sister.'"—*E., p. 69.*

In the Finger Play called "The Nest," Froebel tells the mother:

"The way lies through our imaginative, tender and emotional observation of Nature and of man's life, through the child's taking their meaning into his own heart and expressing by representation what he thus takes in.… The child's sympathy is roused by the young creatures' necessities more than by anything, and chiefly by their nakedness and softness."—*M., p. 149.*

And the action which fosters the growth of sympathy is not to be merely representative; The Garden Song has this motto:

"If your child's to love and cherish Life that needs him day-by-day, Give him things to tend that perish If he ever stays away."—*M., p. 84.*

It is because "the desire for unity is the basis of all true human development" that the child is to be encouraged to help in the work he sees going on around him.

"Family, family—let us say it openly and plainly—you are more than School and Church, and therefore more than all else that necessity may have called into being for the protection of right and property … without you, what are Altar and Church?… Therefore, Mother, in the little finger game, teach your child some notion of the nature of a whole, especially of a family-whole."—*M., p. 159.*

"We have not yet touched nor even considered an important side of child-life, the side of association with father and mother in their domestic duties, in the duties of their calling.… (*E., p. 84*). Do not let the urgency of your business tempt you to say, 'Go away, you only hinder me.' … After a third rebuff of this kind scarcely any child will again propose to help and share the work."—*E., p. 99.*

It is an essential part of the Kindergarten to consider the child as a member of the human family. It is described in one place as:

"An establishment for training quite young children, in their first stage of intellectual development, where their training and instruction shall be based upon their own free action or spontaneity, acting under proper rules … such rules as are in fact discovered by the actual observation of children when associated in companies. (*L., p. 251*).… Practice in combined games for many children, which will train the child, by his very nature eager for companionship, in the habit of association with comrades, that is, in good fellowship and all that this implies."—*L., p. 252.*

Among his Group Instincts Mr. Kirkpatrick mentions the Love of Approbation, and this receives special attention from Froebel at a surprisingly early stage. It is in the "Mother Songs," in connection with his adaptation of an old German nursery rhyme about knights who come to visit "a good child," that Froebel tells the mother that:

"A new life stage has begun, and you, dear Mother, must use your best and most watchful care, when first the child listens to a stranger."

In the same connection he writes:

"The child must be roused to good by inclination, love and respect, *through the opinion of others around him*, and all this must be strengthened and developed.… When, therefore, Mother, observation as to the judgment of others awakes in your child—when, separating himself and on the watch *he brings himself before the judgment of others*, then you really have a double task to perform.…"—*M., p. 190.*

The Love of Approbation cannot be separated from what Mr. Kirkpatrick calls the Regulative, i.e. the Moral and Religious Instincts, for it is both social and regulative, and in the social instincts Froebel sees the foundation of the religious instincts or tendencies, to which we shall come presently. But he also notes a "sense of order," as Mr. Sully does in his delightful "Studies of Childhood," and this he traces back to very early beginnings, connecting it with the tendency towards rhythm.

"That disorder and rough wilfulness may never enter the games, it is a good plan wherever it is possible to accompany each change in the play by rhyme and song; so that the latent sense of rhythm and song, *and above all the sense of order in the human being and child*, may be aroused and strengthened to an impulse for social cooperation."—*P., p. 267.*

One of the earliest Mother Plays, "Tic-tac," deals with rhythmic movement, and in "The

Education of Man" Froebel takes the beginning of "conscious control" still further back. His ideal mother fosters "all-sided life," that is, she fosters the cognitive, emotional and conative, the first by calling the child's attention to his own body and his immediate surroundings, and the second by "seeking to awaken and to interpret the feeling of community between the child and the father, brother and sister," and Froebel goes on:

"In addition to the sense of community as such, the germ of so much glorious development, the mother's love seeks also through movements to lead the child to feel his own inner life. By regular rhythmic movements—and this is of special importance—she brings this life within the child's conscious control when she dandles him up and down on her hand or arm in rhythmic movements and to rhythmic sounds. Thus the genuine natural mother cautiously follows in all directions the slowly developing all-sided life in the child, strengthening and arousing to ever greater activity, and developing the all-sided life within. Others suppose the child to be empty and wish to inoculate him with life, and thus make him as empty as they think him to be."—*E., p. 69.*

It is surprising to find that Froebel, writing so early, has nothing at all resembling any special "moral faculty." His references to "Conscience" are decidedly interesting, though given in quaint connection with games and rhymes for mere babes. He asks why the "Where's Baby?" game gives such delight, and shows his psychological insight in the answer he finds, viz. that it is the feeling or recognition of self, of personality, which gives such joy.

"Why, now, is my child so happy over the hiding game? It is the feeling of Personality which already so delights the child, it is the feeling of recognition of his own self."[35]

The game which follows this repeats the hiding experience, but this time with the cry of "cuckoo," from some one unseen, and this is likened to the conscience call, which is described as "consciousness of union in separation and of separateness, that is personality, in union."—*M., p. 98.*

"In 'Where's Baby Been?' parting and union seem more separate, as though in order that each may become more and more clearly conscious of itself; in 'Cuckoo,' parting and union are, as it were, joined. It is parting in union and union in parting that makes 'Cuckoo' such a peculiar game and so delightful to a child. But consciousness of union in separation, and of separateness—that is personality—in union, is also the essence, the deep foundation of conscience."—*M., p. 197.*

Mr. Kirkpatrick's second Regulative instinct or tendency is that of Religion, but Froebel again, like Mr. McDougall, finds that Religion has its roots in an instinct "not specifically religious,"[36] viz. in the Social Instinct. He says this in "The Education of Man" in the plainest of terms.

"This feeling of Community first uniting the child with father, mother, brothers and sisters, and resting on a higher spiritual unity, to which later on is added the discovery that father, mother, brothers and sisters, human beings in general, feel and know themselves to be in community and unity with a higher principle—with humanity, with God—this is the very first germ, the very first beginning of all true religious spirit, of all genuine yearning for unhindered unification with the Eternal, with God."—*E., p. 25.*

It seems quite in accordance with this that Froebel should write that he likes better the German word *Gott-einigkeit*—union with God—than the foreign word religion; and also that he should speak of "developing the sense of kinship with man in every child, and the sense of kinship with God in every man." So, in his "Mother Songs," he tells the mother to give her child duties to perform, that so he may "feel his kinship" with her:

"Every age, even the age of childhood, has something to cherish that is plain, and from doing so no exemption can be procured; it has therefore its duties. Happy is it for a child if he be led to deal with them adequately, and for the present unconsciously. Duties are not burdens.... Fulfilment of duty strengthens body and mind, and the consciousness of duty done gives independence; even a child feels this. See, Mother, how happy your child is in feeling he has done his small duties. He already feels his kinship with you thereby."—*M., p. 174.*

There is never a separation between Morality and Religion:

"Religion without industry, without work, is liable to be lost in empty dreams, worthless visions, idle fancies. Similarly, work or industry without religion degrades man into a beast of burden, a machine. Work and religion must be simultaneous; for God, the Eternal has been creating from all eternity.... Where religion, industry and self-control, the truly undivided trinity rule, there indeed is heaven upon earth."—*E., p. 35.*

There is only one other instinct mentioned by Froebel, and that is the parental, or, rather, the maternal instinct. He is eager that this should be recognized as an instinct, but he is equally eager that, like other human instincts, its action should be determined by intelligence. In describing the "Plan" for his Kindergarten, Froebel pleads for more careful observation of the child and his relationships, and says that "thereby":

"Deeper insight will be gained into the meaning and importance of the child's actions and outward manifestations and also into the way of dealing with children which has been evolved naturally by the mother led by her pure maternal instinct."—*L., p. 248.*

As to the early beginnings of the instinct in the little girl we can find just a few references, sufficient to show that it did not pass unnoticed, and it seems here legitimate to say that "the girl anticipates her destiny," as Froebel does in speaking of doll-play, though certainly this does not cover all such play:

"The joy of the child in its doll has a far deeper human foundation than is generally supposed—a foundation by no means resting merely in the external resemblance … the girl anticipates her destiny—to foster Nature and life."—*P., p. 93.*

The boy's destiny is "to penetrate and rule Nature," so in the "Mother Songs" Froebel describes how the boy is "cowering that no sign of life in the chicken family may escape him, while the girl starts up, *all her care of things stirred*, in order to beckon or call the hen or cock not to forget their chickens."—*M., p. 143.*

In all his writings, Froebel refers to how much he has learned from mothers: "It was in watching your clever mother-doings that I learnt." But, as he says of himself, it was "a necessary part of me to be irresistibly driven to search out the ultimate or primary cause of every fact of life," and so he writes:

"The natural mother does all this instinctively without instruction or direction; but this is not enough: it is needful that she should do it consciously, as a conscious being acting upon another which is growing into consciousness, and consciously tending toward the continuous development of the human being."—*E., p. 64.*

"Motherly and womanly instinct does much of its own accord; but it often makes mistakes."—*L., p. 63.*

"Women's work in education must be based not upon natural instinct, so often perverted or misunderstood, but upon intelligent knowledge.... Some mothers level the taunt at me that I, a man, understanding nothing of a mother's instinct, should dare to presume to instruct mothers in their dealings with their own children.… How could such a thought enter my head as to attempt anything against the course of Nature? My whole strength is exerted on the contrary, to the work of getting the natural instinct and its tendencies more rightly understood, and more acknowledged; so that women may follow its leadings as truly as possible aided by the higher light of intelligent comprehension, and yet at the same time in all freedom, and with complete individuality."—*L., p. 259.*

So, in what he says of this last instinct, Froebel is faithful to what he has said of all human instincts.

"Man shall assuredly not neglect his natural instincts, still less abandon them, but he must ennoble them through his intelligence and purify them through his reason."

CHAPTER VII
Play and Its Relation to Work

To write even a small book on Froebel without directly touching on the subject of play would be impossible, though in dealing with instincts and the carrying out of natural activities we have necessarily considered much that comes under this heading.

On the educative value of play, Froebel is recognizedly original, and his views have influenced and are influencing schools for young children in most civilized countries. Indeed, it would be difficult to show that modern writers on play, in spite of the scientific thoroughness of their investigations, classifications and terminology, have made much advance upon Froebel's theories. Rather do they tend to show how remarkable was his insight, and how surprisingly well grounded his theories.

Nothing, however, has yet been said as to the relation of play to work, no direct definition has yet been given, nor has any reference been made to the now familiar theories of play.

In Froebel's day, these, as clearly formulated theories, were non-existent. His work was that of a pioneer, and his theory might have been called that of "Preparation through Recapitulation." He would, however, have allowed that play is sometimes, though not always, recreative, and he makes clear the necessity for what he calls "healthy vital energy" (gesunden Lebensmuthe), but he would never have called this mere "surplus energy," because he thought it was not more than was required:

"The genuine schoolboy should be full of life and spirit, strong in body and mind.… Would that, in judging the power of children and boys, we might never forget the words of one of our greatest German writers: that there is a greater advance from the infant to the speaking child than there is from the schoolboy to a Newton! Now, if the advance is greater, the power, too, must be greater; this we should consider."—*E., p. 134.*

Ebers, the Egyptologist, tells us that when he was a boy at Keilhau full provision was made for this abounding energy. We read of walks long and short, of botanizing and geologizing rambles, of climbing trees and cliffs for birds' eggs, of which only one might be taken from a nest. We hear of Indian games out of Fenimore Cooper's Leatherstocking Tales, of classic and other dramas on winter evenings, and of Homeric battles, which Froebel, he says, would have called "signs of creative imagination and individual life." There was swimming and skating and coasting and "the spacious wrestling ground with the shooting stand and the gymnasium for every spare moment of the winter"; and a piece of ground "assigned to each pupil, where he could wield spade and pickaxe, roll stones, sow and reap." But the great game was the Bergwacht, where the boys, divided into four parties that all might be active, actually constructed, and then attacked and defended stone fortresses. "How quickly," says Ebers, "we learned to use the plummet, to take levels, hew the stone and wield the axe." The weapons were blunted stakes. It was forbidden to touch the head, but it was a point of honour among the boys to yield as prisoner if touched by the pole, "and what self-denial it required!" These combats were held on fine Saturday evenings, and when all was over "the women," probably the girls of the school community, had lighted fires and made supper ready, and the lads slept in their fortresses while two sentinels marched up and down, relieved every half-hour. On the Sunday following the boys were not required to go to church, "where we should merely have gone to sleep."

It has frequently been brought as an accusation against Froebel that he makes no clear cut distinction between work and play, and that is true, but who nowadays does? Common sense would probably join hands with the philosopher in saying that the feeling of freedom is the chief distinction of play as opposed to work, and this is the definition quite distinctly given by Froebel. The definition is given in his detailed enumeration of "the various directions of an active life of instruction and education," and after mentioning religious training, cultivation of the body as the means of expressing mind, the study of Nature, etc., etc., he comes to:

"Play, that is, spontaneous representation and exercise of every kind."—*E., p. 236.*

Another definition given in "The First Action of a Child" is:

"Play, which is independent outward expression of what is within."—*P., p. 29.*

It is because it is spontaneous that Froebel calls play, during the period of earliest childhood, when the child is gaining control of language, "the highest phase of human development at this stage."

"Play and speaking form the element in which the child lives at this time.… Play is the highest stage of child-development, of human development at this stage, because it is spontaneous (freithätige) representation of the inner, representation of the inner out of the need and desire of the inner itself. This is implied in the very word Play."—*E., p. 34.*

For modern views on play we turn to the exhaustive study made by Karl Groos in his two volumes, "The Play of Animals," and "The Play of Man." Here we find the writer taking "the conception of impulse life as a starting-point," and reaching the conclusion "that among higher animals certain instincts are present which, especially in youth, but also in maturity, produce activity that is without serious intent, and so give rise to the various phenomena which we include in the word 'play.'" In this play, Groos goes on, "opportunity is given to the animal through the exercise of inborn dispositions, to strengthen and increase his inheritance in the acquisition of adaptations to his complicated environment, an achievement which would be unattainable by mere mechanical instinct alone." In the treatment of human play he considers "an analogous position is tenable," but, for the word instinct, with its particular reactions, he must substitute "natural or hereditary impulse."

We have already seen that though Froebel recognized the existence and importance of human instinct, still he distinguished between it and the "definite and strong instincts" which belong to the animals lower than man. We have seen that he regarded the play of childhood as "spontaneous self-instruction" based on the instincts of investigation and of construction or representation, action being regarded as the principal means of investigating, as well as of gaining control over the surroundings and over the self. We have noticed, too, that Groos feels inclined to assume a universal "impulse to activity," and points out that Ribot approaches such an assumption, though for himself he can only venture to "hold fast to the fact of the primal need for activity." Froebel does, as we have seen, attribute to the infant the one instinct of activity, which in one place he calls "the natural longing for some mode of activity inherent in all children," and this he says becomes differentiated at a later period.

The special place given by Groos to imitation as "the link between instinctive and intelligent conduct" is also noteworthy. For we have seen that Froebel regards imitation in precisely the same light, never calling it an instinct, but saying that it is the outcome of spontaneous activity, and that it leads on to understanding.

"For what man tries to represent or do he begins to understand."—*E., p. 76.*

"As now, habit in the child proceeds from spontaneous and independent activity, so also does imitation; ... the whole inner life of the child shows itself as a tri-unity in the three-#fold phenomenon of spontaneous activity, habit and imitation."—*P., p. 28.*

It is impossible to make plain how Froebel regarded play, until it is known how he regarded work, work, too, not only for a child but for a human being. What he desired for all was work which produces joy; he calls it "a debasing illusion that man works, produces, creates, only in order to preserve his body, only to secure food, clothing and shelter." Man, he says, works "primarily and in truth that his real essence may assume outward form," and one of his sayings is that "the true spirit of life is the genuine spirit of play." In an ideal state of affairs, no human being would be condemned to entirely mechanical work. Work "worthy of the nature of man" is to Froebel work which in some way expresses the man; mechanical work is dismissed as "degrading man into a beast of burden or a machine." It is because man is of God that he must work, must produce. "Nearer we hold of God who gives, than of his tribes who take, I must believe," is Froebel's thought in Browning's words:

"Each thought of God is a work, an act, a result.... God created man in His own image. Therefore man must create and work like God. Man's spirit must hover over the unformed and move it that figure and form may come forth. This is the higher meaning, the deep significance, the great purpose of work and industry, of working, and, as it is truly significantly called, of creating. We become like God by diligence and industry, by work and action, which are accompanied by the clear perception or even the least anticipation that thereby we represent the inner by the outer; that we give body to spirit and form to thought, make visible the invisible, give an outward transient existence to the eternal that lives in the spirit.... Early work, guided in accordance with its inner meaning, confirms and elevates religion. Religion without work is apt to become empty dreaming."—*E., p. 30.*

"The boy is to take up his future work which now has become his calling, not indolently in sullen gloom, but cheerfully and joyously, trusting God, himself and Nature, rejoicing in the manifold prosperity of his work.... Nor will the father say that his son must take up his own business ... he will see that every business may be ennobled and made worthy of man."—*E., p. 233.*

It is too cheap a jibe to throw at Froebel and his educational theories that he makes little distinction between work and play. It ought never to come from any one who has made even a slight study of psychology. The sting is meant to lie in the suggestion that play is trifling and easy and that it requires no exertion, while work is serious and demands concentrated effort, but this view will not bear any consideration. Every one knows that the play even of an adult, where the differentiation between work and play ought to be more possible, is often most exhausting, either to body or to mind. As to the play of childhood, one of the best known passages in "The

Education of Man" is the one in which Froebel protests that:

"Play at this time is not trivial, it is highly serious and of deep significance."—*E., p. 55.*

It is in this passage, too, that he speaks of the child "wholly absorbed in play," who after "playing enduringly even to the point of fatigue" has fallen asleep "while so absorbed," and calls this "the most beautiful expression of child-life at this stage."

It is Froebel's glory that as early as 1826 he had applied the theory of development to education and, rightly or wrongly, he believed that if we could but supply to our school children material suited to their needs according to their stage of development, they would respond with the same eagerness that the younger child shows in what we call his play, but what Froebel called his "self-culture and self-education." He states this view quite distinctly:

"We have considered the object and aim of human life in general.... It now remains to show in what sequence and connection the life impulses of the boy develop at this stage, how and in what order and form, the school should work in order to satisfy human instincts in general, and especially the instincts of the boy at this stage of school-life.

"From a consideration of *the means of instruction and manner of teaching thereby conditioned, which necessarily coincide with the striving of man toward development*, what is necessary for the knowledge of number, of space, of form, of exercises in speech, of writing and of reading comes out clearly and definitely."—*E., p. 229.*

The view that "the material of instruction and the manner of teaching" are necessarily conditioned by the child's stage of development is a view that has rapidly gained ground. Froebel did his best to apply it, and it had a partial application in the "culture epochs" theory of the Herbartians. It has received a stronger impetus into what seems at present a much truer direction, from the experimental work carried out at Chicago, under the auspices of Professor Dewey. Froebel maintained that it was a condition of satisfactory work in every subject. For example, in connection with the teaching of writing he says:

"Here, as in all instruction, we should start from a definite need of the boy, a need, which must, to a certain extent, have been previously developed, if he is to be taught with profit and success. This is the source of a multitude of imperfections in our schools, that we teach without having awakened any need for it, nay even after having repressed what need was already there! How can instruction and the school prosper?"—*E., p. 223.*

Froebel speaks in the same way of work in colours, saying "children feel the need of a knowledge of colours." Of poetry in general, including religious verses and prayers, he says "these must be given according to the requirements of the development of the child's mind, and must give expression to what is already there."

Returning now to the subject of play as such, we find that Groos retains as "general psychological criteria of play," but two "of the elements popularly regarded as essential—namely, its pleasurableness, and the actual severance from life's serious aims." Of these he says: "Both are included in activity performed for its own sake."

It is in connection with very young children that Froebel speaks of activity for its own sake, and here he does not differentiate between work and play. He is true to his theory that in all things capable of development, "what is definite proceeds everywhere from what is indefinite." So he says that:

"Play is at first just natural life."—*E., p. 54.*

He maintains that:

"The activity of the senses and limbs is the first germ or bud, and play, building and shaping (Gestalten) the first tender blossoms of the formative instinct, and that this is the point of time, at which man is to be prepared for future industry, diligence, and productive activity."—*E., p. 34.*

But, in the case of the boy a little older, though still only seven or eight, Froebel does distinctly differentiate, giving the definition of play already quoted, "spontaneous expression and practice of every kind," and saying of work, that:

"Boys of this age should have definite domestic occupations, indeed they could be actually instructed by mechanics and farmers as has already been done by many a father with active natural insight. Boys of a somewhat advanced age should be often placed in a position to accomplish something with their own hands and their own judgment ... should devote daily at least one or two hours to an occupation with outward results ... after such a refreshing *work bath*, I cannot better designate it, the mind goes with new life to its intellectual employments."—*E., p. 236.*

Of the infant, Froebel writes:

"At this stage of development the man-to-be (dem erschienenen werdenden Menschen) *uses his body, his senses, his limbs, entirely for that use, practice and exercise, not at all for its results*, to which he is quite indifferent, or, to speak more correctly, of which he has as yet no idea. Out of this comes what begins at this stage, the child's play with his limbs; with his hands, fingers, lips, tongue and feet, and also with the movements of his eyes and of his face."—*E., p. 48.*

Of the older child Froebel very distinctly insists that he wants more than the activity, that he wants outward result. But the result of which he speaks is one which Groos himself would not disallow. It is only the outward product of the impulse which has been gratified, a result which is present to the mind of the older child, while to the infant no such consciousness is possible.

"What at an earlier stage of childhood was action for the sake of the activity, is now, in the boy, activity for the sake of the visible result; the child's instinct of activity has developed into an instinct for shaping or giving form, and herein lies the solution of the whole outer life or outer manifestation of boy life at this stage."—*E., p. 99.*

Inquiring into the kind of pleasure derived from play, Groos finds that it rests primarily on the satisfaction of inborn impulses, which press for discharge, and he gives three special "inborn necessities which ground our pleasure in play—namely, the exercise of attention, the demand to be an efficient cause, and imagination."

As to attention, he suggests that it lends a meaning to the vague idea of a general need for activity, speaking of "the pitiable condition of boredom" if opportunity is withheld.

Froebel, of course, has much to say about the instinct of activity, or, as he usually calls it in "The First Action of a Child," the instinct of employment (Beschäftigungstrieb), which is noticeable "even when the so-called three months' slumber has just ended." He, too, frequently refers to "the ennui and pernicious lack of occupation," to the "mischievous idleness which results from our not satisfying or misdirecting the natural longing for activity inherent in all children." It is because Froebel's thoughts always run on conscious revelation of the self within as the explanation of human life, that he makes so much of "the child's instinct to employ itself" (Triebe des Kindes, sich zu beschäftigen). This also explains how so much that he says corresponds with what Groos brings forward with regard to "the joy in being a cause," and its modifications. These modifications are (*a*) pleasure in the mere possession of power, (*b*) emulation, when a model is copied, and (*c*) in the case of imitative competition there is pleasure in surpassing others as well as the enjoyment of success resulting from that pleasure of overcoming difficulties which comes under the combative instinct.

Froebel is warning parents that they must provide for their children opportunity for the exercise of the impulse to formative activity by letting them help, even if their help is really a hindrance, and he says:

"If his earlier activity was only imitation of what he saw around him, now it is sharing in the business of the house, lifting, pulling, carrying, digging, and wood-splitting. In everything the boy will exercise, measure and compare his strength that his body may grow stronger, *that his power may increase, and that he may know its measure....* At this age the healthy boy, brought up simply and naturally, never avoids a difficulty, never goes round a hindrance: no, he seeks it out and overcomes it. 'Let it lie,' calls the vigorous youngster to the father, who offers to remove an obstacle; 'Let it lie: I can get over it.' ... As activity gave pleasure to the child, so work gives pleasure to the boy. Hence the daring feats of boyhood.... Easy is the most difficult, without peril the most adventurous, for the impulse comes from the innermost nature, from his heart and will."—*E., p. 101.*

"But it is not only the impulse to use and to measure his power that urges the boy to roam and to climb—it is the need to widen his mental horizon.... The same desire holds him to the plain ... he occupies himself with water and with plastic materials. For he seeks now *because of the feeling of power over material already gained* to master these. Everything must serve his impulse towards construction.... And so each forms for himself his own world, *for the feeling of his own power demands his own space and his own material....*"—*E., pp. 102-107.*

"But all the plays and occupations of boys do not by any means aim at representing objects and things. On the contrary, *in many pure exercise of strength and measuring of strength predominate*, and many have no further aim than the display of strength. Yet the play of this age has always its peculiar characteristic, namely, as during the period of childhood, the aim of play consisted simply in activity as such, so now its aim is always a definite conscious purpose, which characteristic develops more and more as the boys increase in age. This is observable even with all games of bodily movement, of running, boxing, wrestling, with ball-games, goal, hunting, and war games, etc."

"*It is the sense of sure and reliable power, the sense of its increase* both as an individual and as a member of the group *that fills the boy with all-pervading jubilant joy* during these games."—*E., p. 113.*

It is evidently difficult even for practised thinkers to grasp the importance of what we so glibly call play in the case of the young child. Mr. Kirkpatrick, for instance, fully recognizes its importance in regard to children somewhat older, and he makes a suggestive distinction between play and amusement, calling play active, while amusement is passive. Others, he says, work for our amusement. But when he speaks of the infant, he slips into the mistake of saying that the infant, even though active, "amuses" itself. To the ordinary observer the whole life of a young child is play, but it would be as correct to say that it is all work.

Professor Stout, true to what he calls the tendency of the moderns to see in the little child what is writ large in the adult, allows "purely intellectual curiosity" on the part of the infant. We have no right to call an infant passive and therefore amused even when the mother shakes the rattle for his edification. He may be striving hard to accommodate his organs of sight, he may be recalling previous sounds similar and dissimilar, he may be watching and comparing different movements and different positions. He has so much to learn "with the world so new and all," and, to judge from his seriousness, it is at times a most momentous inquiry. The baby to whom the activity of throwing is new, and who spends full twenty minutes in throwing a tram ticket on the floor of the car—which the patient mother restores each time—throwing, too, with such force and evident purpose, cannot properly be said to be playing. Nor can the infant who stares with such concentration at the lighted lamp and who, when the mother moves out of the direct range of the light, strives with all its feeble strength to readjust its position to that entrancing brightness.

Of the very young child, Froebel writes:

"The first voluntary employments of the child are observation of its surroundings, spontaneous taking in of the outer world, and play, which is independent outward expression … it is evident therefore how important is the training … and also the kind of voluntary playful occupation of the child.… For as the life of man is continuous one can recognize even in the first baby life, though only in the slightest traces and most delicate germs, all the mental activities which in later life become predominant."—*P., p. 29.*

When Groos reaches the pedagogical standpoint, he says:

"We have repeatedly found in the course of this inquiry that even the most serious work may include a certain playfulness, especially when enjoyment of being a cause and of conquest are prominent. Between flippant trifling, and conscientious study there is a wide chasm which nothing can bridge, but not all play is such trifling. Who would forbid the teacher's making the effort to induce in his pupils a psychological condition like that of the adult worker, who is not oppressed by the *shall* and *must* in the pursuit of his calling, because the very exertion of his physical and mental powers in work, involving all his capabilities, fills his soul with joy? Since play thus approaches work, when pleasure in the activity as such, as well as its practical aim, becomes a motive power (as in the gymnastic games of adults), so may work become like play, when its real aim is superseded by enjoyment of the activity itself. And it can hardly be doubted that this is the highest and noblest form of work."[37]

It is beyond dispute that this is the kind of work that Froebel desired for all humanity, so it is not surprising if he drew no hard and fast line between work and the "*play*" which he insists "*is not trivial*," and which he urges parents to protect and guide. Of play at the stage of boyhood he writes:

"Joy is the soul of every activity at this period."—*E., p. 304.*

And in reference to the right kind of instruction he says:

"The union of school and life is the first and indispensable requirement … if men are ever to free themselves from the oppressive burden and emptiness of merely extraneously communicated knowledge, heaped up in memory, if they would ever rise to the joy and vigour of a knowledge of the real nature of things, to a living knowledge of things.… Mankind is meant to enjoy a degree of knowledge and insight, of energy and efficiency, of which at present we have no conception; for who has measured the limits of God-born mankind! The boy is to take up his work which has now become his calling, not indolently in sullen gloom, but cheerfully and joyously."—*E., pp. 230-233.*

One distinct line of division is that drawn by Groos when he says that with young animals and probably with children "their first manifestation of what is afterwards experimentation, fighting and imitative play, etc., is rarely conscious, and therefore we cannot assert with assurance that it is pleasurable."[38] In this case he says the biological but not the psychological germ of play is present. Froebel never lost sight of the psychological point of view in so far as his desire always was to see what the action meant to the actor, what the child's play meant to the child, and also in that he desired all the activity to be joyous, to be performed for its own sake. But it was really the biological view that he endeavoured to reach and to set forth.

Coming now to the Theories of Play, it seems clear that, if he had ever heard of them, Froebel would have endeavoured to combine those of Recapitulation and Preparation. He states quite plainly that these are not incompatible, recognizing that in any work or play, by which the child retraces past stages of human development, he gains what is most necessary for his own future life, control over his surroundings as well as over himself, something after the manner in which these have been gained by the race.

"The observation of the development of individual man and its comparison with the general development of the human race show plainly that, in the development of the inner life of the individual man, the history of the mental development of the race is repeated, and that the race in its totality may be viewed as one human being, in whom there will be found the necessary steps in the development of individual man."—*E., p. 160.*

"Indeed each successive generation and each successive individual human being, inasmuch as he would understand the past and present, must pass through all preceding phases of human development and culture, and this should not be done in the way of dead imitation, or mere copying, but in the way of spontaneous self-activity."—*E., p. 18.*

"Man should, at least mentally, repeat the achievements of mankind, that they may not be to him empty dead masses, that his judgment of them may not be external and spiritless; he should mentally go over the ways of mankind, that he may learn to understand them. However it may be said of this growing activity of boyhood, which by spirit and law are destined for a conscious aim, 'My son does not require this.' Perhaps you are right, I do not know, but you do know that your sons need energy, judgment, perseverance, prudence, etc., and that these things are indispensable to them; and all these things they are sure to get in the course indicated...."—*E., p. 282.*

It is often said that traditional games are mere survivals, degenerate imitations of ancient customs, and therefore not worth encouraging. But children are not bound by tradition, and Froebel is probably right when he says:

"It is my firm conviction that whenever you find anything that gives children lastingly and ever freshly a joy belonging to a true pure life—anything where innocence and mirth predominate—you have found something which has at the bottom of it a higher and more important meaning for a child's life."—*M., p. 172.*

We cannot always tell why children enjoy the game, or what they gain from it. Such games are at least the earliest and simplest introduction to "the rules of the game," and they contain the elements of choosing sides and of whispered secrets. These things may seem small to the ordinary onlooker, but not to the real observer, who sees the amount of self-control required by a child of four or five, that he may not proclaim the secret aloud, the difficulty he has in whispering, and the importance to him of the choice between oranges and lemons or whatever it may be. There are certainly some which most thinking persons, Froebelian or otherwise, would wish to discourage. As Froebel himself said of some that he found in use:

"I thought some were too empty and silly and some said a great deal that I would not willingly have said to children. Yet the counting games themselves seemed to me important in many ways, as I hope will appear from comparing the way I have dealt with them, and above all, as the mottoes are meant to point out. I even wished to keep the sound of the well-known popular words, at least in the opening words...."—*M., p. 157.*

Certainly, Froebel would have had no dealings with either work or play which would interfere with progressive development, he wanted recapitulation because he regarded that "great necessary highway" as the road to sure progress.

"Only if in each particular we tread again the great necessary highway of humanity as a whole, does the great and vigorous early life of humanity come back to us in and through the children."—*E., p. 222.*

"Education must be much more tolerating[39] and following than predetermining and prescribing, for by the full application of the latter method of instruction we should entirely lose the characteristic, the sure and steady progressive development of mankind."—*E., p. 10.*

Some educators who have made much of the "culture epochs" might have avoided mistakes and exaggerations if they had taken to heart Froebel's repeated warning that the child has "living relations" not only with the past, but with the future, besides being at the same time the child of the present generation.

"Parents should view their child in his necessary connection, in his obvious and living relations to the past, present, and future development of humanity, in order to bring the education of the child into harmony with the past, present and future requirements of the development of humanity and of the race…. Man, humanity in man, as an external manifestation, should therefore be looked upon not as perfectly developed, not as fixed and stationary, but as steadily and progressively growing, in a state of ever-living development, ever ascending from one stage of culture to another toward its aim, which partakes of the infinite and eternal.

"It is unspeakably pernicious to look upon the development of humanity as stationary and completed and to see in its present phases only repetitions and greater generalizations of itself. For the child, as well as every successive generation, becomes thereby exclusively imitative, an external dead copy—a cast, as it were, of the preceding, and not a living ideal of the stage which it has attained in human development considered as a whole, to serve future generations in all time to come."—*E., p. 17.*

Underlying all that Froebel has to say of play, is the idea that it is a preparation for future life activities. This is implied even in the definition given of the play of the child of three years old, viz. that it is "spontaneous self-instruction"; it is most evident in the passage:

"Play, building and modelling are the first tender blossoms, and this is the period when man is to be prepared for future industry, diligence and productive activity."—*E., p. 34.*

"The whole later life of man has its source in the period of childhood, be this later life bright or gloomy, gentle or violent, industrious or lazy, rich or poor in action, passed in dull stupor or in keen creativeness, in stupid wonder or in intelligent insight, productive or destructive."—*E., p. 55.*

Of his later institution, the Kindergarten, Froebel says:

"The great end and aim of the whole undertaking is the Education of Man from its earliest beginning, by means of action, feeling, and thought, in accordance with his own inward being and outward relations, … *this to be attained by* the right care of child-life, *the encouragement of childish activities.*"—*L., p. 164.*

"For the object is twofold: Firstly the realization in as clear and perfect a manner as possible, of *the fundamental conception of a mode of education* based upon the early and complete training of human life, and *satisfying the needs of children by a genuine encouragement of their spontaneous activity* through the medium of a normal institution which we have symbolically named a Kindergarten."—*L., p. 166.*

About the play of boyhood Froebel says:

"Play to the boy is a mirror of the combat of life awaiting him in the future: therefore, in order to strengthen himself for the combat, the human being both in early and later boyhood seeks out obstacles, difficulty and combat in his play…. Many of his actions have an inner significance.... How wholesome it would be if parents and child, for their present and future, if parents believed in this, if they would observe the life of their children in this respect, what a new living bond would unite parents and child, what a new thread of life would be drawn between their present and their future life!"—*E., p. 118.*

Of his own Keilhau boys he writes:

"One thing is certain, these plays are the outcome of the spirit of boyhood. And the boys who played thus were good scholars, intelligent, and willing to learn, seeing and expressing clearly, diligent and full of zeal. Some are now capable young men with well trained heads and hearts, quick in expedients and dexterous in action; some are capable, clear-sighted men, and others will become so."—*E., p. 111.*

In America at least the authorities are beginning to realize the truth of Froebel's words as to the importance of playgrounds, and actual experiment has shown that he was right in saying that "even the plays should be under right guidance," not for purposes of repression, but for the encouragement of real play which "must necessarily break forth in joy from within."

"Justice, moderation, self-control, truthfulness, loyalty, brotherly feeling and again, strict impartiality—who, when he approaches a group of boys engaged in such games, could fail to catch the fragrance of these delicious blossomings of the heart and mind and of a firm will; not to mention the beautiful, though perhaps less fragrant, blossoms of courage, perseverance, resolution, prudence, together with the severe elimination of indolent indulgence? Flowers of still more delicate fragrance bloom ... forbearance, consideration, sympathy and encouragement for the weaker, younger and more delicate; fairness to those who are as yet unfamiliar with the game.

"Would that all who, in the education of boys, barely tolerate playgrounds might consider these things! There are, indeed, many harsh words and many rude deeds, but the sense of power must needs precede its cultivation. Keen, clear and penetrating are the boy's eyes; keen and decided therefore, even harsh and severe is his judgment of those who are his equals, or who claim equality with him in judgment and power.

"Every place should have its own common playground for the boys. Glorious results would come from this for the entire community. For at this period, games, whenever it is feasible, are common, and thus develop the feeling and desire for community and the laws and requirements of community.

"The boy tries to see himself in his companions, to feel himself in them, to weigh and measure himself by them, to know and find himself with their help. Thus the games directly influence and educate the boy for life, awaken and cultivate many civil and moral virtues."—*E., p. 113.*

It was in watching boys one day—"boys," he says, "of the right age for these plays, but whose life is not awakened, or has been dulled, and who now idly lounge around, getting in their own way, as it were"—that a friend said to him, "I do not understand how these boys cannot play, how many plays we had at their age!" And it is here that Froebel gives his version of the "surplus energy" theory when he writes:

"In every case the plays of this age are or should be pure manifestations of strength and vitality, they are the product of fullness of life, and of pleasure in life. They presuppose actual vigour of life, both inner and outer. Where these are lacking, there cannot be true play, which, bearing life in itself, awakens, nourishes and heightens life.... This shows clearly that even the plays at this age should be under guidance[40], and the boy made ready for them, i.e. his life, his experience both in school and out of it, must be made so rich that it must necessarily break forth in joy from within, like the blossom from the swelling bud. Joy is the soul of every activity of boyhood at this period."—*E., p. 303.*

It is here, too, in the section entitled, "Play or Spontaneous Expression and Practice of Every Kind" that Froebel begins a general classification of boy's play:

"The plays, or spontaneous occupations, of this age are of three kinds, they are either (*a*) imitations of life, or (*b*) spontaneous applications of what has been learned, or they are (*c*) perfectly spontaneous expression with all kinds of material. These last are either governed by the material, or by the thought and feeling of the human being.… They may be and are either Physical plays, exercising strength and dexterity, or else mere buoyancy of life; or Sense plays exercising the hearing, e.g. in hiding games, etc., or the sight, as in shooting plays or colour plays, etc.; or Intellectual plays, games of reflection and judgment, e.g. draughts, etc. As such they are already arranged, but the true aim and spirit of the play is rarely understood and the games are seldom managed according to the needs of the boy."—*E., p. 304.*

This general classification is very much the same as that of Groos, who divides Play first into two main classes, viz. Playful Experimentation and Playful Exercise of the Second or Socionomic Order. Under the first heading come I. Playful Activity of the Sensory Apparatus; II. Playful Use of the Motor Apparatus; and III. Playful Exercise of the Higher Mental Powers. The first two correspond to Froebel's Sense Plays and Physical Plays, and the third to his Intellectual Plays. Under the second heading, Groos brings Fighting Plays, which as we have seen Froebel attributes to the unconscious desire to measure and increase strength; Imitative Play, which to Froebel is the child's way of learning by action; Love Plays of which Froebel takes no notice at all, and Social Play. Under this comes what has been given as to the importance of Playgrounds, and much of what Froebel wrote as to the Kindergarten Games. For instance, as part of the work of the students in his Training Course comes:

"The acquisition of little games arranged to exercise the limbs and senses of the child.… The acquisition of other games arranged to suit special ends and suited to varied grades of development.… Practice in combined games for many children, and particularly action games, which will, from the first, train the child (by his very nature eager for companionship) in the habit of association with comrades, that is, in good fellowship and all that this implies.… To games for individual children succeed games for the whole Kindergarten together. The child in these associated games alternately appears first as taking some individual or separate part, and then as merely one of several closely knit and equally important members of a greater whole, so that he becomes familiar with both the strongly opposed elements of his life; namely the individual determining and directing side, and the general ordered and subordinated side."—*L., p. 253.*

Games of this kind have been much misused, especially by being given a rigidity of form which, Froebel wrote:

"Would quite destroy that fresh merry life which should animate the games … the games would cease to be games and lose their full educational power. The main thought must be held fast; but the precise form and style in which the games are played must be the outcome of the moment. The freer and more spontaneous the arrangement, the more excellent is the effect of the game."—*L., p. 85.*

The number and variety of plays and games noted by Froebel is quite surprising. Of the long list given by Groos there are few indeed which he does not mention.[41] The plays for older children are given in "The Education of Man," but other games encouraged at Keilhau are to be found in the accounts given by Ebers. Even in his earlier work Froebel shows how closely he had been observing the play of little children, but this he worked out later in his Mother Songs, in the papers on his various "Gifts," and in that on Movement Play. These later books were written and the play material was planned because Froebel saw that the children who do not play are those "in whom life has not awakened or has been dulled," just because "the true aim and the spirit of play is rarely understood and the games are seldom managed according to the needs of the boy."

CHAPTER VIII
Froebel's Play-Material and its Original Purpose

To one who believed, as Froebel did, that "the means by which the child gains his first ideas of his own nature and life and the nature and life of the cosmos, are his play and playthings," these playthings could not be indifferent.

"It has been stated as a fundamental truth that the plays and occupations of children should by no means be treated as offering merely means for passing, we might say for consuming, time, hence as mere outer activity, but rather that by means of such plays and employments the child's innermost nature must be satisfied."—*P., p. 108.*

Froebel was speaking of his own Play-material—known by the name of "Froebel's Gifts" because he thought them the most suitable gifts for little children—when he wrote:

"To realize his aims, man, and more particularly the child, requires material, though it be only a bit of wood or a pebble with which he makes something or which he makes into something."—*P., p. 235.*

And although his opinion of the importance of that particular series of playthings, which he chose from among those he saw in general use, may have been exaggerated, still there is a good deal of sound psychology in what he says about them. In speaking of imitative action and construction, we have already touched upon what were perhaps the most important ideas underlying this series.[42]

"What presents are most prized by the child? Those which afford him a means of unfolding his inner life most freely and of shaping it in various directions."—*P., p. 142.*

But Froebel also writes of his Gifts that "they will cover the whole ground of training in sense perception," and he has managed to think out a very fair number of the points which Dr. Ward, in his Analysis of Perception, notes as important.

One of Froebel's frequent Reviews of his play-material begins:

"How has the child developed up to this point? How has the world, the objects and things around him developed? How has the child developed himself *especially through the toys*—the means of play and employment—which have thus far been given him? The brightening light in the child's mind illuminates the objects around him. In proportion as the inner light increases, the nature of external objects grows clear to him … the law of development is that of progress from the unlimited to the limited, from the whole to the part, from an undifferentiated to a membered totality … the outer world comes to meet the inner world, it does not hinder, but helps the inner world.

"The man advanced in insight should be clear about all this before he introduces his child to the outer world. Even when he gives his child a plaything he must make clear to himself its purpose, and the purpose of playthings and occupation material in general. This purpose is to aid the child freely to express what lies within him—to bring the phenomena of the outer world nearer to him, and thus to serve as mediator between the mind and the world."—*P., pp. 169-171.*

Then Froebel explains in so many words the really psychological aim or meaning of his sequence of "Gifts," so well known by name—and even better known in most *un*-psychological practice—but little understood in their real and original significance, as a means of perception, the earlier ones at least, for children much below even Kindergarten age.

"Recognizing the mediatorial character of play and playthings, we shall no longer be indifferent either to the choice, the succession, or the organic connection of the toys we give children. In these I offer them, I shall consider as carefully as possible, how the child may in using them develop his nature freely and yet in accordance with law (laws of mind), and how through such use he may also learn to apprehend external things correctly and to employ them justly. As the child's first consciousness of self was born of physical opposition to and connection with the external world, so through play with the ball, the external world itself began to rise out of chaos and to assume definiteness. In recognizing the ball the child moved from the indefinite to the definite, from the universal to the particular, from mere externality (compare Prof. Ward's 'mere thing stuff') to a self-included space-filling object. In the ball, especially through movement, through the opposition of rest and motion, through departing and returning, the object came forth out of general space as a special space-filling object, as a body: just as the child by means of his life (activity) also perceives himself, his bodily frame, as a space-filling object, as a body. The child has thus obtained two important terms of comparison for his first intellectual development; body and body, object and object.... At the same time there begins in the child, as in a seed-corn, a development advancing towards manifoldness. For this reason he should receive a corresponding seed-corn in the object which he first detaches as object from the external chaos. Such object should, like himself, include an indefinite manifoldness, and be susceptible of a progressive development. Such an object is the ball (Gift I)."—*P., p. 171.*

The very first "intimation of an intellect," Froebel writes, is when the child is seen to "keep his gaze fixed upon the motion of a bright object. This begins a few weeks after birth." The ball is to be given to the baby "when the starting-point of recognition and knowledge (Erkennens und Erkenntniss), viz. perceiving, noticing, thinking (das Gewahrwerden, das Bemerken und Beachten) becomes perceptible": when the child "can freely move its little arms and hands, when it can perceive and distinguish tones, and can turn its attention and gaze in the direction from which these tones come."

In his analysis of Perception, Dr. Ward distinguishes (i) Assimilation or Recognition, (ii) Localization or Spatial Fixation, and (iii) Objective Reference, or Intuition of Things. Of these, the first, Assimilation, has already been taken up in Chapter IV, and we have seen that, according to Dr. Ward, it involves Retention and Differentiation, though in itself there is no active comparison, and we have seen that Froebel also spoke of the earliest impressions as "almost imperceptible, but *fixed* by repetition and by change,"[43] and of a "perception of sequence" involving "dim" or "unconscious comparison."

Of the second process Dr. Ward writes: "To treat of the localization of impressions is really to give an account of the steps by which the psychological individual comes to a knowledge of space," and he goes on to say that psychologists may have been too apt to examine "the conception of space and not our concrete space perceptions." Now Froebel did consider concrete space perception, and with a certain amount of care. That he saw its importance is clear from the fact that in discussing his "means of employment" he says:

"They will cover the whole ground of training in sense perception but *will begin with the observation of space and the knowledge that comes from that, since the child first feels and finds himself in space and finds others occupying space around him.* They are to go on by development of limbs and senses and by means of language to understand Nature in all directions, so that finally man *who at first could find himself only in space and by means of space*, may learn to know himself as an existent, feeling, thinking, intelligent, rational being, and as such to try to live."—*P., p. 19.*

And although Froebel may not fully have realized that, as Dr. Ward puts it: "The infant's earliest lessons in spatial perception are in exploring his limbs," still we do find him writing from Blankenburg, in a letter accompanying the first sketch of his Nursery Songs:

"I soon felt that some important connecting link was imperatively required to prepare the newly awakening life of a child for its later activity with the ball. It was through the ball itself that I discovered this link: in general terms it may be described as *the first development of muscular movement and sensation* specially distinguishing infancy. The link between the infant, still an undivided self-sufficient whole of peaceful life, and the ball, which is something external given to him to play with, lies in the child's own limbs, the child's own senses; and *the first toys and occupations of the child come from himself; he plays with his own limbs*, and uses them as the material for representing his ideas. This spontaneous activity of limb and vividness of sensation natural to infancy must also be studied; for a considerable degree of cultivation of these powers is already necessary in the use of the ball, etc.... To help the child to use his own body, his limbs and sensations, and to assist mothers to a consciousness of their duties ... I have carefully preserved several little songs and games and send this collection to you for your severe criticism."[44]—*L., p. 108.*

Having said that "the child first perceives himself, his corporeal frame, as a space-filling object, as a body, by means of his life," or his activity, the first two of this collection naturally deal with large body movements. In the one the mother alternately lowers and raises the infant, "letting him really feel a slight shock," and in the other the baby tramples with his feet, and she is told to supply the object of resistance. This resistance, as we have seen, gives him "the dim consciousness of self, which comes out of physical opposition to, and connection with, the outer world," which Dr. Ward speaks of under the head of Localization of Impressions. Dr. Ward writes that "the distinction between his own and foreign bodies begins when the child feels the difference between a series of movements accompanied by passive touches, and one without passive touches," but Froebel goes no further than noting what comes through "resistance." The ball, however, as we have just seen, is to be used so as to assist the child's comprehension of "a self-included space-filling object," and through play with the ball he is to gain the "three great perceptions of object, space and time."

In the Intuition of things, Dr. Ward distinguishes five points "concerning which psychology may be expected to give an account: (*a*) the reality; (*b*) solidity or occupation of space; (*c*) permanence, or, rather, continuity in time; (*d*) unity and complexity; and (*e*) substantiality and the connection of its attributes and powers."

(*a*) *Reality* he disposes of as "not strictly an item by itself, but a characteristic of all the items that follow." Of (*b*), *Solidity or Impenetrability*, he writes that "here our feelings of effort come specially into play. They are not entirely absent in those movements of exploration by which we attain a knowledge of space; but it is when these movements are definitely realized, or are only possible by increased effort, that we reach the full meaning of body as that which occupies space." Dr. Ward goes on to add as "in the highest degree essential," that muscular effort should meet with something which seems to be "making an effort the counterpart of our own."

Besides telling the mother to give the required definite resistance, by opposing her hand or chest to the little trampling feet, Froebel gives a "new play, a new perception of the object," when he tells the mother that "as soon as the child is sufficiently developed to perceive the ball as a thing separate from himself," she should tie a string to it and pull gently.

"The child will hold the ball fast, the arm will rise as you lift the ball, and as you loosen the string the hand and arm will sink back from their own weight; the feeling of the utterance of force, as well as the alternation of the movement, will delight the child. From this, however, soon springs a quite new play, that is also something new to the child, when, through a suitable drawing and lifting, the ball escapes from the child's hand and then quietly moves freely before him as an individual object. Through this play is developed in the child a new feeling, the new perception of the object as a something now clasped, grasped and handled, and now as a freely active opposite something."—*P., p. 36.*

Unity and Complexity, "the remaining factors in the psychological constitution of things," says Dr. Ward, "might be described in general terms as the time-relations of their opponents...."

And Froebel, going straight on from "the opposite something," comes in like manner to time-relations.

"One may say with deep conviction that even this simple activity is inexpressibly important for the child, for which reason it is to be repeated as a play with the child as often as possible. What the little one has up to this time directly felt so often by the touch of the mother's breast—union and separation—it now perceives outwardly in an object which can be grasped and clasped. Thus the repetition of this play confirms, strengthens, and clears in the mind of the child a feeling and perception deeply grounded in, and important to the whole life of man—the feeling and perception of oneness and individuality, and of disjunction and separateness; also of present and past possession.... The idea of return or recurrence soon develops to the child's perception, from the presence and absence; that of reunion from the singleness and separateness; of future repossession from present and past possession, and so the idea of being, having and becoming, are the dim perceptions which first dawn on the child.

"From these perceptions there at once develop in the child's mind the three great perceptions of object, space and time, which were at first one collective perception. From the perceptions of being, having and becoming in respect to space and object, and in connection with them, there soon develop also the new perceptions of present, past and future in respect to time. Indeed, these ninefold perceptions which open to the child the portals of a new objective life, unfold themselves most clearly by means of his constant play with the one single ball."—*P., p. 36.*

Dr. Ward gives as the first step "in the psychological constitution of distinct things"—as opposed to what he calls "mere thingstuff"—"the simultaneous projection into the same occupied space of the several impressions, which we thus come to regard as the qualities of the body filling it."

Froebel writes:

"We gave, therefore, to the mother the brightly coloured soft ball to make a unity of touch and perception through sight, for through the brightness it makes itself known to sight, and through warmth (softness?) to touch, as an objective phenomena, a thing in itself."—*P., p. 65.*

To reach unity and complexity, says Ward, "it is essential that objects should recur, and recur as they have previously recurred, if knowledge is ever to begin." The constituent impressions must also "be again and again repeated in like order to prompt anew the same grouping," and the constancy of one group must present itself "along with changes in other groups, and in the general field.... It is only where a group, as a whole, has been found to change its position relatively to other groups, and—apart from causal changes—to be independent of changes of position among them, that such complexes can become distinct unities and yield a world of things."

Froebel writes of one of his early plays:

"It is really important for the human being, especially as a child, that the essential perceptions of things should be *repeated frequently* under different forms, and *if possible in a particular order*, so that the child may easily learn to distinguish the essential from the unessential and accidental, and the abiding from the changing. Unnoticed and unrecognized though the phenomena are to the child, yet the impression of them will be certain and firm, and this so much the more when the repetition has been precise and clear."—*P., p. 88.*

Later, speaking of a child's earliest attempts at walking, he says:

"The smallest child who begins to exercise the power of walking, loves to go from place to place—i.e. *he likes to turn about and to change the relationships in which he stands to different objects, and in which they stand to him. Through these changes he seeks self-recognition and self-comprehension, as well as recognition of the different objects which surround him, and recognition of his environment as a whole.*"—*P., p. 243.*

Dr. Ward requires still more and says that "the unity of a thing" carries us over to temporal continuity, and this he attributes to "the continuous presentation of such a group as the bodily self, which makes us infer continuity of existence, for presentations which have been presented, removed and re-presented."

We have seen already that Froebel says the child perceives the ball "through departing and returning, as a space-filling object, as a body, just as he perceives himself, his corporeal frame, as a space-filling object, as a body." And there is also a quaint, but interesting reference to something of this kind in one of the earliest Nursery Songs called "All Gone," where the mother is distinctly told that she must help her child to realize continuity through change.

"How can the child understand what you mean when you say 'It's all gone, Baby'? He will not be contented unless you put meaning into it. What he saw just now he sees no longer, what was above is below, what was there is just now vanished. Where, then, has it gone?"

And the baby is supposed to be quieted by the mother's playful tale of the present whereabouts of his bread and milk, a German version of the homely "Down red lane."

Professor Ward's last point in the intuition of things is "substantiality." "What is it," he says, "that has thus a beginning and continues indefinitely?" The answer is that "of all the constituents of things only one is universally present, that of physical solidity, which presents itself according to circumstances, as impenetrability, resistance or weight.... In other words, that which occupies space is the substantial; the other real constituents are but its properties or attributes, the marks or manifestations which lead us to expect its presence."

Froebel, again, sums up the ideas he intends the child to gain from play with the ball:

"The ball shows contents, mass, matter, space, form, size and figure; it bears within itself an independent power (elasticity) and hence it has rest and movement, and consequently stability and spontaneity; it offers even colour, and at least calls forth sound; it is indeed heavy—that is, it is attracted—and thus shares in the general property of all bodies.... Therefore, it places man, on his entrance into the world, furnished with activity of limbs and senses, in the midst of all phenomena and perceptions of Nature and of all life ... to place man through a skilful education in the understanding of Nature and life, and to maintain him in it with consciousness and circumspection cannot be done too early."—*P., p. 53.*

The soft ball of the first gift is supposed to be given to the child when he is three or even two months old, but when he reaches six or eight months, he is supposed to be ready for something which "makes itself known especially through noise, sound, tone, as it were through speech." The second gift therefore consists of a wooden sphere and a cube, which are intended not only to please the child by the noise they make, but to serve as material for comparison. The mother is told to roll the sphere and then, in order to make this oppositeness between sphere and cube perceptible to the child, to place the cube steadily before him and presently to take one of his little hands, pushing gently at first, but

"finally overcoming the gravity of the cube and pushing it away with the child's hand and fingers … drawing the child's strength, although yet so feeble, into the play, that his limbs may be trained, his strength increased, and that he may experience and perceive much through his own activity."—*P., p. 77.*

By even these few representations the mother can present to her child:

"The quiet, firm sure-standing on a relatively larger surface; the filling of space by each object; heaviness which is expressed by pressure; the final overcoming of heaviness (gravity); and the possibility of moving away the body by the use of a proportionately greater strength. The perception of all these and many other facts, showing themselves merely as changing phenomena in oft-recurring repetition, will give pleasure even to the child who is scarcely half a year, or at least not a whole year old, especially when the play is placed in intimate connection with the child's life, and with his impulse to activity."—*P., p. 78.*

Many plays are suggested, all to be accompanied by song or rhyme, only, says Froebel, "one must not go on in opposition to the wish of the child, but always follow his requirements and needs and his own expressions of life and activity."

It is in this connection that Froebel notices how early a child begins to note cause.

"Even the child whose capacity for speech is as yet undeveloped will remark the cause of the fall of the cube, at least experience has shown us that children of this age drew away the holding support, and, as the cube then fell over, turned toward their mother with face and body as in joyous triumph."—*P., p. 80.*

The sphere and cube are also to be compared as to shape:

"Through all that has been done hitherto, the child's attention has been predominantly called to the object, as filling space, and acting, but only incidentally to the object as being the identical one; nor yet to the figure and shape, nor to the members and parts. But attention to the form and figure of the object can also be utilized for the child in play."—*P., p. 83.*

So the mother is directed to hide the cube in her hand and show it again—so that the child will watch for its reappearance.

"By this play the child is not only again made to notice that the cube fills space, but his attention is also called to its precise form; and he will look at it sharply, *unconsciously comparing* it with the hand to which his eyes were first attracted."—*P., p. 84.*

"Each object speaks constantly to man by its qualities and attributes, and still more to the child, though in mute speech…. It is essential for the intellectual development of man that the surroundings should speak to him by their qualities and attributes."—*P., p. 95.*

Froebel's "Gift III" is a little box containing eight-inch cubes for building purposes, and after the child has clearly gained the idea of "outer object" Froebel says:

"Let us first of all hasten to place ourselves together in the children's play corner, and there seek to discover what attracts the child, or, rather, in what direction he himself turns his attention, what he would like to do and what he needs for the purpose. Let us take our place there as quietly and as unnoticed as possible, observing how the child, between the ages of one and three years, after he has clearly gained the idea of "outer object," has contemplated the form and colour of the self-contained body which he can handle, has moved it here and there in his hands, and experimented upon its solidity, now tries to pull it apart, or at least to alter its form in order to discover new properties in it, and to find out new ways of using it. If the little one succeeds in his attempt to separate the object, we see that he then tries to put the parts together, to form the whole which he had at first, or to arrange them in a new whole. We see that he will unweariedly and quietly repeat this for a long time.

"Let us linger over this significant phenomenon and seek to recognize through it what we have to furnish to the child from inner grounds and without arbitrariness. This is: something firm which can be easily pulled apart by the child's strength, and just as easily put together."—*P., p. 117.*

The time when the child wants this something to arrange is given as any time "between the ages of one and three." It is the time when "his greatest delight consists in the quick alternation of building up and tearing down."—*P., p. 106.*

At first the little one will be satisfied with arranging and rearranging the cubes, piling them one upon another, "placing one before, behind, beside another." Soon, however, he will try to make something definite, and "the intelligent nurse interprets the dim idea and sees whether a something, a table, a chair, etc., can be perceived in what is represented." Then the something must have a purpose, so the chair is grannie's chair, the table is ready for the soup, and so on.

There is nothing here which is not quite a usual proceeding. Froebel's peculiarity of treatment comes from his desire to give the blocks to the child as a whole which he can take to pieces. This is the reason of the traditional proceeding, perhaps still kept up in old-fashioned kindergartens, when the children first slip the lid out a little way, then reverse the boxes, pull out the lid and lift it off the box. The directions are Froebel's own, and are given:

"in order to furnish to the child at once clearly and definitely, the impression of the whole, of the self-contained; from this perception, as the first fundamental perception (Grundanschauung) all proceeds and must proceed."—*P., p. 123.*

It is clear that this meaning is quite lost when the same proceeding is forced on older children, who are quite accustomed to pull down and build up.

Froebel emphasizes the fact that the pieces are of the same cubical form as the whole thus presented, and adds:

"Thus fundamental perceptions, whole and part, form, and size, are made clear by comparison and contrast, as well as deeply impressed by repetition."—*P., p. 119.*

It is in speaking of this simplest of toys that Froebel enters a strong protest against the complex and useless toys which afford no scope for childish activity.

"Here, then, we meet a very great imperfection and inadequateness—indeed in reference to the inner development of the child an obstructing element in that which is now so frequently provided as a plaything for children; an element which slumbers like a viper under roses—it is, in a word, the already too complex and ornate, too-finished plaything. The child can begin no new thing with it, cannot produce enough variety by means of it; his power of creative imagination, his power of giving form to his own idea, are thus actually deadened. For when we provide children with too finished playthings we at the same time deprive them of the incentive to perceive the particular in the general, and of taking the means to find it.… What presents are the most prized by the child as well as by mankind in general? Those which afford him a means of unfolding his inner life most purely and of shaping it in a varied manner, giving it freest activity and presenting it clearly."—*P., p. 122.*

This quotation sets forth quite plainly the main idea underlying all the varied toys or play-material known as the "Gifts and Occupations" of the Kindergarten.

According to Mr. Hailmann and other writers, the gifts are material by which the child can gain ideas, and the occupations furnish material for gaining skill. But Mr. Hailmann allows that this distinction, which to him seems important, was never formulated by Froebel.

Froebel's psychological knowledge, in fact, was in advance of that of his interpreters. He knew that it was by action, by manipulation of material, that the child gains his ideas and that the clear distinction between gift and occupation which to Mr. Hailmann is "very important" is on the contrary actually non-existent.

Gifts III to VI are boxes of building blocks, intended to present sequence in difficulty of manipulation, and also increasing variety of form. Because of the stress he laid on self-expression, Froebel thought very highly of the educational possibilities of a box of bricks. In "The Education of Man" he writes:

"Look into this education room of eight boys, seven to ten years old. On the large table stands a chest of building blocks, in the form of bricks, each side about one-sixth of the size of actual bricks, the finest and most variable material that can be offered a boy for purposes of representation. Sand or sawdust, too, have found their way into the room, and fine green moss has been brought in abundantly from the last walk in the beautiful pine forest. It is free time, and each one has begun his own work. There in a corner stands a chapel … there a building which represents a castle.…"—*E., p. 108.*

After the bricks come the coloured tablets of Gift VII, which children from four and upwards, *if left free*, often highly appreciated as material for making patterns; and the Sticks or splints of various lengths of Gift VIII, with which they used to lay outlines of familiar objects. English children often use burnt matches for this, sometimes they do the same thing with "mother's pin-box," and a child quite innocent of Kindergarten ideas has been seen to appropriate the various nails of a tool-box to the same purpose. Along with the sticks Froebel supplied rings of metal or paper; the little English child who used the nails took small curtain rings for the petals of her flower and screw nails for its stalk. In Gift IX the child is presented with very small articles for stringing or arranging—beads, coloured beans, pebbles, etc. A child's pleasure in this material and in the sticks and rings probably shows that he is ready to practise movements of the thumbs and forefingers. Froebel said that the use of these sticks called the child's attention to "linear phenomena," and I have already mentioned that many years ago, when we were still using Froebel's play-material, I heard a child call out, "Oh, I'm making lines!" just after he had been using the sticks. The other children contentedly went on rubbing with the crayons; but this young discoverer continued to make laborious lines, always from left to right, till the work was completed to his satisfaction.

The remaining "Gifts" include coloured paper to fold and cut either to produce such objects as boats, boxes, purses, chairs, etc., or to form patterns, or to weave together for the well-known paper mat; drawing and paper materials; modelling clay and sand, and so on.

The weakness of the series is the semi-psychological semi-mathematical arrangement, which has been dealt with in the following chapter. What Froebel meant to do was to pick out from among the material he saw given to children, or appropriated by them, those things which seemed to him best adapted to call out the activities of children at various ages or stages, in accordance with his idea that "the man advanced in insight should make clear to himself the purpose of playthings, viz. to help the child to express himself, and to bring the phenomena of the outer world nearer to him."

Surprise has often been expressed that Froebel did not include such toys as dolls in his series.

One reason is that he did not live long enough, for he does speak of doll-play and says that later the time will come "when we shall speak of the doll and the hobby-horse as the plays of the awakening life of the girl and of the boy." In his brief reference he does speak of the child's own nature becoming objective through the doll-play, and he adds that by such play she "anticipates and feels her destiny." He notes, too, with interest that:

"Little girls make their favourite dolls of the heavy bootjack or like piece of wood. I was informed by a mother that a heavy sandbag which she accidentally found became her most cherished doll, because it had in it the weight of an actual child, and so she gave herself up to the illusion and imagined herself to be carrying a real child."

Undoubtedly Froebel was right in demanding simple toys and in characterizing the "too complex toy" as a "viper under the roses," and also in demanding that toys should be carefully considered and chosen so as to meet the needs of the child's developing mind. But the plays and the toys of a developing child cannot be definitely prescribed, and every similar attempt is likely to fail, as Froebel's has done. In his choice, Froebel was biased by the great idea which obsessed him, the idea of development. Like all human beings, he had the defects of his virtues, and it is to these defects that we must now turn our attention.

CHAPTER IX
Weak Points Considered

An honest attempt to show what credit is due to Froebel, for the remarkable anticipations of modern theories on which he based his pedagogy, seems to involve the opposite process of inquiring whether or not any of his practices can be shown to have an unsound basis.

The modern boys' school, with a few, and a very few exceptions, does not even approach the school at Keilhau as a place of real education, as any one may see who reads the account given of it by Georg Ebers. On the other hand, the modern Kindergarten is probably in many ways an advance upon the original attempts. Many practices of which Froebel approved are now discarded, some no doubt because of progress in physiological discovery; we know now that a child is not fitted as regards nervous development and muscular control to deal with fine pricking or drawing in chequers.

But a better knowledge of physiology does not account for all the changes that have taken place. Important as they undoubtedly were in Froebel's eyes, the modern Kindergartener is inclined to smile over her predecessors' "worship of the 'Gifts'"; and, though we are agreed as to the importance of games, the modern teacher chooses from a wide, perhaps too wide a range, and no longer reposes blind faith in certain circle-games with their supposed "symbolic" virtue.

To some, the word symbolic will at once suggest Froebel's weakest point, others will resent any such idea, for symbolism appeals strongly to one and repels another. For Froebel himself, undoubtedly the whole world was symbolic, in so far as he regarded the universe as one expression of the Divine. To him, as to Browning:

"The earth has speech of God's writ down, no matter if In cursive script or hieroglyph."

But this has not affected his educational practice to the extent generally supposed.

At the same time it does seem as if one, if not two, psychological errors lie at the root of certain practices which the modern Froebelian has discarded.

It would be most unfair to Froebel not to emphasize what is often overlooked, viz. that the "Gifts" were important in his eyes solely because he believed that in them he was presenting toys, or "play-material," exactly suited to the succeeding stages of the child's development, bodily and mental. "The new gift," he says, "corresponds both to the child's increasing constructive ability, and to his growing capacity to comprehend the external world." And he writes:

"But such a course of training and occupations for children answering to the laws of development and the laws of life, demanded a thoroughly expressive medium in the shape of materials for these occupations and games for the child: therefore to meet this point I have arranged a series of play materials under the title of: 'A complete series of gifts for play.'"—P., p. 250.

It should also be noted that Froebel did not commit the mistake of inventing new toys. What he attempted to do was what we are all attempting now, viz. to use what natural instinct has already selected, as a basis for conscious educational work. Balls and building blocks, coloured tablets and papers, sand and clay, are all spontaneously appropriated by normal children. Even these materials which seem to us unchildlike are not so in different surroundings. For instance, in the Black Forest, one may watch children playing with long slivers of wood exactly like Froebel's laths, and these they take from the cut logs which are being hauled up for winter storage.

Again, it is only fair to point out that Froebel's followers have appropriated material which he suggested as suited to children aged from three months to five or six years, and have used them with children from four or five to six or seven and even older.[45] Teachers have also found it convenient to disregard Froebel's frequent warnings not to interfere, to let the child "bang and pound" when he wants to, to let him "play quietly and thoughtfully by himself as long as he will," to give him "the greatest possible freedom of expression." In some, at least, of the original text-books on Kindergarten practice, written by Froebel's early disciples, this advice is totally disregarded, and we find prescribed the most formal of object lessons, dealing with the properties of the ball in set questions and answers; only at the end comes "If there is time, the children may be allowed to roll the ball."

Still, when all due allowance is made, there remains the fact that Froebel attributed far too much importance to the series of toys he arranged, and in addition to this he must be held in large measure responsible for the extraordinary amount of mathematical perceptions of which young children have been considered capable, and beneath which many gleams of intelligence may have been extinguished.

The psychological error which seems to underlie both these mistakes in pedagogy seems to have been that of making too much of the outer factor in the process of perception. Froebel was quite right and quite modern in refusing to draw any hard and fast line between sense perception and thinking, in saying that the child moves "from perception of a thing, joined with thought about it, up to pure thought." But he must have failed somehow, sufficiently to grasp the fact that all that is present to sense is not necessarily perceived, that perception depends not merely upon what is presented, but upon previous mind content. The word "apperception," though apparently somewhat fallen into disfavour of late, has certainly been of service in emphasizing this point.

What seems strange is that in the very book, in which we find the theory disregarded in practice, we find Froebel stating the theory itself in the plainest of terms:

"The properties and nature of the outer world unfold themselves in exact proportion to the capacities of the child."—*P., p. 120.*

"The child creates his own world for himself; it is at once the expression of his inward realization of the external world and its surroundings, and also the outward representation of his internal mental world, the world of his own subjectivity."—*L., p. 141.*

"Above all, it is the old within the new, which clarifies, unfolds and transmutes itself, thus developing what is new.... We must not require of the child anything not conditioned by his previous achievements."—*P., p. 169.*

No one, surely, can maintain that these words are carried into effect in e.g.:

"Could forms of knowledge (mathematical forms) be, for a child of one to three, play forms, and thus forms produced by spontaneous activity? Well, why not? Arrange the eight part-cubes together, and say, 'One whole.' But divide it immediately and say, 'Two halves.'… Or, comparing and connecting and describing by song at the same time that the objects are manipulated:

'Look here and see! One whole two halves. One half two fourths, two halves four fourths. One whole four fourths. Four fourths eight eighths. Eight eighths one whole.'"—*P., p. 138.*

There is certainly no "old within the child" of one to three, which can condition this achievement, nor is there any spontaneity. For the child a little older we have:

"The hints that are here given suffice to show that the knowledge forms are adapted to children of three and four years of age, and that they incite plays which are both spontaneous and nourishing to heart and intellect.… These few indications for the use of these forms must suffice; they already show sufficiently clearly that the observation and comprehension of them are perfectly suited to the active, intellectual and emotional sides of children three and four years of age, and to actual free play which strengthens intellect and feeling."—*P., p. 185.*

Now the "hints" refer to making clear to the child, always in justice, be it remembered, in the concrete, "as perceptible facts only," such points as "similarity of size with dissimilarity of shape and position, in such words as:

"Twice as long and half as wide, Half as long and twice as wide, The same size are we two."

Certainly children differ very much, and some have a special aptitude for mathematical relations, but to most children under five these words would convey nothing. *Half* may have a meaning, though at that age and for some time after we hear of "a fair half" and "quarter" is generally used as a name for any fraction recognized as not a half, even if it should be greater. Such words as *fourth* and *eighth* can have no meaning for a child who shows no consciousness of difference when shown six, seven or eight objects. At the age of three, an average child recognizes three objects, but when a fourth is added, he proceeds to count one by one, he does not recognize three plus one.

Again, we must repeat that Froebel never intended any mathematical ideas to be forced upon unwilling children. He constantly tells the mother not to force, and he frequently speaks of the child's "accidental productions which will become a point of departure for his self-development," through the explanatory rhymes, to be sung by the mother in order to call the child's attention to the results of his own action. It is true, too, that it is in connection with this kind of work, or play, that Froebel writes of "the knowledge-acquiring side of the game, which is the quickly tiring side."

But the fact remains that either Froebel made a miscalculation as to what mathematical ideas are within the grasp of children of tender age, or else he attributed too much consequence to what is outside. It is indeed quite possible to present to a child of any age, by means of the cubes of his Fifth Gift, several particular instances of the Theorem of Pythagoras, as Froebel suggests. But though the construction is present to the sense of both child and adult, the career of the child of five or six, who perceives or apperceives the relationship of the squares so presented, may be watched with interest. He is likely to distinguish himself in mathematical research, should he live long enough. Froebel ought to have known, indeed he did know, for he taught it to others, that the child does not "quickly tire" of acquiring knowledge suited to his stage of development by methods equally suitable. From the houses and railway trains, of which at this stage they seem never to tire, children probably gain as much knowledge as Nature means them to absorb by such means. In Froebel's own hands, with his real and sympathetic understanding of the need for freedom of action, probably no harm was done, but it is easy to see how the ordinary teacher would grasp at the possibility of producing mathematical prodigies through what was supposed to be play.

The same error seems to show itself in various ways, e.g., in some of the reasons Froebel gives for choosing his First Gift, though there is no fault to be found with the choice. He was right in saying that the child first takes in a whole, not a variety of elements, to be combined later. Because of this fact, the ordinary coral and bells, with all its complexity, is just as much a whole to the infant as the woollen ball. But Froebel does seem to have thought that he must make the "outer objects," or toys from which the child is to gain his earliest ideas, as simple as these ideas, and this certainly implies a wrong view of perception. The same objection might be taken to Froebel's directions as to how the Third Gift—an 8-inch cube, cut once in each direction—is to be presented; how in order "to furnish to the child clearly and definitely the impression of the whole, of the self-contained, from which fundamental perception everything must proceed," the box is to be reversed, the lid slipped out and the box is to be lifted "that the play thing may appear as a cube closely united." But in this case Froebel is "presenting" the first divided unit, "something which may be taken to pieces, arranged and re-arranged and finally re-constructed," for it is "by this dismembering and re-constructing, and perception of real objects that true knowledge and especially self-knowledge comes to the child."

A second psychological error, or at least an inconsistency, seems to lie at the root of certain practical directions Froebel gives with regard to the use of his toys. In spite of his iteration and re-iteration that the child's mind is a unity, that though separation is "permitted for the thinking mind," there is none in reality, yet in his anxiety for the due fostering of the whole, of the "doing, feeling and thinking" his harmonious development, in actual practice he has an attempted separation which has had bad results. A Kindergarten practice, now discontinued, was to make the children build, either on different occasions, or during different parts of one lesson, what Froebel called (*a*) Life-forms or Objects (Lebens oder Sachformen), i.e. houses, churches, etc.; (*b*) Beauty or Picture forms (Schönheits oder Bildformen), i.e. symmetrical designs; and (*c*) Knowledge or Instruction forms (Erkenntniss oder Lernformen), i.e. squares, triangles, etc. Though this classification is based on the familiar and important "knowing, willing and feeling," yet it is plain that a child may experience quite as much emotion, probably more, in building a house as in making a star pattern, and that the active side is involved in every kind of construction. Froebel draws a parallel, legitimate to a certain extent, between intellect, feeling and will on the one hand, and truth, beauty and usefulness on the other. Here, however, we can quote him against himself; "Separation is only permitted for the thinking mind." The useful ought to be beautiful, there is beauty in all truth, and the æsthetic revelation of the world is the world in order. Beauty degenerates into mere ornament and artificiality, when separated from life and use. "Mathematics," as Froebel wrote himself, "is neither foreign to life, nor deduced from life; it is the expression of life as such: its nature may be studied in life, and life may be studied with its help.… Mathematics should be studied more physically and dynamically as the outcome of nature and energy."—*E., p. 206-7.*

The result of this suggested separation has in past times been disastrous. Failing to recognize that a young child is of necessity exercising his intellectual power in constructing his castle or bridge of blocks, and failing still more to realize that ornament is far from synonymous with beauty, teachers have wearied and stupefied children with mathematical forms for which they were not ready, and have forced upon them symmetrical designs when their souls hungered for "puffer trains."[46]

It is easy to show that what Froebel wanted was only due attention to what we now call the affective and conative as well as to the intellectual. From the very first he insists on this, and justly, though his way of doing it may seem to us quaint. About the child's imitation of the clock he writes:

"As soon as the child's first capacity for speech is somewhat developed, we notice how he tries, in and by the movement, to listen to the tone and to imitate it with the tone of his own voice. *Tic tac*, we hear him say, imitating the movement of the pendulum; *pim paum* (ding dong?) he says when the sound is more noticed.… So we must observe that even when he first begins to speak the child expresses and retains the physical part of the movement by *tic tac*, but by *pim paum* he perceives the movement more, if one may say so, from the feeling in the mind, and if I may be allowed so to express myself, by the 'here and there' which comes later, the child catches hold (festhalten) of the movement more as a thing of comparison, of recognition, and in his dawning thought, more intellectually.… It is most important that the mother should observe the first and slightest traces of the articulation (Gliederung) of the child as an active, emotional and intellectual being, and watch it in his development from existence to experience and thought, so that in his development no side of his nature should be cultivated at the cost of the others, nor should any be repressed or neglected for the sake of the others. It seems important, and we believe that all who quietly observe the child have remarked, or will yet remark, that from the first the child expresses the swinging movement in a singing tone, in a tone which approaches song and so serves the emotional nature. Thus early is it shown that the real foundation, the starting-point for the education of humanity and so of the child, is the heart and the emotions (das Gemüth u. die Gemüthliche), but that training to action and thought (zur That u. zum Denken), the physical and the intellectual goes with it side by side constantly and inseparably. Thought forms itself in action, and action clears itself in thought, but both must have their roots in the emotions."—*P., p. 41.*

Two further reasons may be given for Froebel's belief in his selected series of toys: (*a*) his delight in the theory of development, and (*b*) his eagerness to bring the child as soon as possible to that consciousness of self which differentiates man from the lower animals.

Every sign of unity of plan within the universe gave Froebel real joy, and he traces development from the simple to the complex, from the undifferentiated to the differentiated, not only in plant and animal life, but also in the inorganic. Much of what he says on crystals may be fanciful, but much is beautiful and suggestive. "Chemical combination" is to him "the life of the inorganic world," and he writes:

"We have in this a new confirmation of the law of development in crystals, the passing from special-sidedness to all-sidedness, from imperfection to perfection as the law of all development in nature. Man, then, appears as the most perfect earthly being, in whom all that is corporeal appears in highest equilibrium and in whom the primordial force is fully spiritualized, so that man feels, understands, and knows his own power. But while man externally and corporeally has attained equilibrium and symmetry of form, there heave and surge in him, viewed as a spiritual being, appetites, desires and passions.

"As in the world of crystals we noticed the heaving and surging of simple energy, and in the vegetable and animal worlds, the heaving and surging of living forces, so here the heaving and surging of spiritual forces. Therefore man with reference to spiritual development has returned to a first stage as crystals are in a first stage with reference to the development of life.… For this reason the boy should at an early period be taught to see Nature in all her diversity as a unit, as a great living whole, as a thought of God. The integrity of Nature, as a continually self-developing whole must be shown him at an early period."—*E., p. 198.*

Although this particular passage was written in connection with Nature Study for older boys, yet it is from thoughts such as these that Froebel seems to have taken an idea that man-in-infancy ought to meet, if it may be so expressed, matter-in-infancy. Though everything in the surroundings was to help to bring about self-consciousness, "the air blowing about all living creatures, as well as the arousing spiritual language of words," yet that definite thing-in-itself, which is to help the child to an early dim consciousness of self is to be "the counterpart of himself," a simple undifferentiated whole "susceptible of a progressive development."

And now we must come to the question of Froebel's "Symbolism," a thorny subject, because one into which the personal equation enters largely. Some writers, notably Miss Susan Blow, author of "Symbolic Education," regard this symbolism as all-important, Froebel's glory rather than his weakness. Others consider that it appeals to adults alone and that where it is supposed to affect children it tends towards artificiality and sentimentality. In so far as this is true, it must be regarded as a weak point.

It is, however, not an easy task to settle what ideas are covered by the term "Froebel's symbolism." The dictionary meaning for symbol is "a visible sign or representation of an idea; anything which suggests an idea, as by resemblance or convention; an emblem; a representation; a type; a figure; as the lion is the symbol of courage and the lamb of meekness or patience."

It certainly passes my comprehension how anything can symbolize an idea not yet acquired, however much it may help in calling up ideas already more or less clearly gained. The crown may symbolize power to an adult, but not to the child, who when told that Stephen and Matilda fought for the crown, innocently inquired: "Couldn't they have had another one made?" The Union Jack may symbolize British nationality or British freedom, or even British Jingoism to adults who already possess these ideas, but not to a little child. On the other hand, any kind of celebration appeals to children, as to more primitive people, and to be allowed to march round the playground on Empire Day carrying a flag arouses a joyous emotion, which will later be interwoven with patriotic ideas of various kinds. It is decidedly open to question whether as regards the child Froebel himself intended much more than this, whatever his followers may have done.

Professor Thorndyke gives us to understand that Froebel says a child plays with a ball because it symbolizes "infinite development and absolute limitation." Now it is true that Froebel wrote in his "Aphorisms"—quoted in a footnote to Hailmann's "Education of Man"—"The spherical is the symbol of diversity in unity and of unity in diversity.... It is infinite development and absolute limitation." But the "Aphorisms" were not written for children, and Hailmann quotes the passage in speaking of Froebel's philosophical doctrines as to the ultimate nature of force and matter!

To Froebel, Spirit is everywhere striving for utterance. The Universe—the Manifold—is the revelation of one great mind, and everything in Nature, "though soundless it be to the ear, a message can give emblematic (sinnbildlich) but clear." Certainly, he would have the boy study Nature, "the writing and book of God," but it is not to the boy that he says:

"The works speak, by the form the Spirit manifests itself. By that which has been produced and created, the nature and spirit of the producer and creator make themselves known. The world must therefore necessarily manifest the nature of its original cause—the spirit of its Creator."

For Froebel as for Goethe, the Time Spirit "weaves for God the garment we see Him by." He calls "the temporal an expression of the eternal, the material a manifestation of the spiritual." He speaks of "the Power which reveals itself by uniting all things, in Nature in the Universe as weight, in human life as Love," and it pleases him to put into the hand of the boy—in that picture of a family group by which he typifies Humanity—a ball hanging by a string, and this he calls an emblem or symbol (Sinnbild).

There is nothing in all this with which any one need quarrel. Froebel was assuredly an idealist, but in these days that is no longer a term of reproach. No one, to whom it does not appeal, need use the suggestion, but to those of us who believe that right guidance of a child's delight in fairy tales is one way of developing his sense of reverence, there is nothing so very far fetched even in Froebel's way of trying to bring to the child's consciousness, the spirit striving for utterance not only in every beautiful form, but in everything beautiful as he does in "The Smell Song."

Of fairy tales Froebel says:

"The child, like the man, would like to know the meaning of what happens around him. This is the foundation of the Greek choruses, especially in tragedies. This, too, is the foundation of many legends and fairy tales, and it is the result of the deeply-rooted consciousness of being surrounded by that which is higher and more conscious than ourselves."—*P., p. 147.*

So, when the child delights in the scent of the flower, Froebel says to the mother: "Let your child find in all things a mind, a struggle for being. Colour form and spicy smell all forthtell the One ruling hand which called all into existence." But all she is told to pass on to the child is only the thought that an angel has put the scent there and is saying: "The little one does not see me, but without me there would be no fragrance."

Although in one sense the educator of young children need have no dealings at all with "symbolism," yet in another, a walking-stick does, for the boy who bestrides it, symbolize, a horse, as a piece of wood may symbolize for his little sister the infant whom she may nurse and caress, with what Froebel calls "the dim and transferred perception of inner life." Here Froebel seems quite right, as when in speaking of a child's visit to a toyshop he says, "a true child is content with very little of the outer, he is satisfied by a doll or cart, a whistle or a sheep, provided only that in or through it he can find his own world and represent it in actual deeds."—*M., p. 199.*

It may be said, too, that there is symbolism in children's drawings, the animal or object is symbolized by that which to the child is the most outstanding characteristic. One small boy drew a camel with a rider so small that some one protested he could not see over the hump, so the artist promptly drew a second rider in front. Being asked if he could draw an elephant, he assented cheerfully and added a trunk to his camel. By the addition of claws the elephant became a cat, but at that point he paused, remarking, "It's not very like a cat, it's more like a bird," and a pair of wings completed the transformations. In like manner by help of a walking stick a child becomes his own father, and a pair of spectacles transforms him into his grandmother. But in all such cases the child is dealing with ideas he has already grasped.

To say that circle or ring games help a child to gain an idea of unity—Ring a Ring of Roses may give the first dim idea of corporate unity—is a very different thing from saying that a circle is to the child a symbol of unity. This is the kind of thing, however, that Froebel is supposed to have said, but after careful investigation one is surprised to find how little there is, and to what extent Froebel's disciples and translators seem to have read in their own interpretations.

For instance, in searching for passages about symbolism, we find in the English translation of the paper on Movement Plays, a passage stating that the "Snail Game" forms a frequent conclusion to a "games" period, because it yields the form of the circle, "which is symbolic of wholeness." On comparing this with the original, however, we find that this phrase is an addition of the translator's. No doubt she considered it explanatory, but all that Froebel himself says is that the game is suitable "because it finally unites all the players in a lively and completely finished whole." To practical teachers, who know the difficulty of getting a number of children to settle down after a game, this may bear a very different meaning.

It seems to me that Froebel's translators have been altogether too fond of the word "symbolic." The German words usually translated "symbol" and "symbolic" are "Sinnbild" and "Vorbild," with their respective adjectives. After considering innumerable passages in which these words occur it seems plain that Froebel's meaning would often have been better expressed by "typical," or by "significant," and sometimes by "metaphorical."

For instance, it is quite legitimate to say of such perceptions as Froebel intended a child to gain from his second "Gift"—resistance, weight, hardness and softness, noise, etc.—that the ball and cube give, and are only intended to give, "normal, fundamental and *typical* perceptions" (nur die normalen, begründenden und vorbildlichen Anschauungen), and Froebel goes on to say that the same perceptions must come from many other objects. There is nothing *symbolic* here, and there is no reason for using this word.

That in many passages *significant* would be a much more correct translation than symbolic is abundantly evident. Froebel was convinced, and most people will now agree with him, that there is real meaning or significance in those activities, which are common to children of all countries, and this meaning he endeavours to discover. Small blame to him if, though wonderfully correct on the whole, he sometimes hits upon a wrong meaning, in which case we are apt to fall back upon that convenient scapegoat, his symbolism.

In one of his letters he thanks his cousin for describing to him how she had watched a tiny child "who quietly let his eye travel from the ball hanging at the end of its cord, up to the hand which held it," and he adds:

"I am convinced, and I wish that all teachers, and especially all mothers, shared in the conviction, that the very earliest phenomena of child-life are *full of symbolic meaning*, that is to say, they indicate the higher, the intellectual life in the child and his individual peculiarities at the same time. Our duty is to search in everything for its ultimate basis, its point of origin, its well-spring; and to make clear the connection between the outward manifestation and its inward cause."—*L., p. 101.*

What Froebel deduced from the incident was that the child looks not only at the appearance of the swinging ball, but for the cause of the swinging phenomenon, the supporting, moving hand. So it is plain that for "full of symbolism" we should here read "full of significance." Or, again, in his excellent sketch of early boyhood, with its desire to share the work of the father, its desire to explore, to collect, to construct, etc., Froebel concludes:

"Thus it is certain that very many of the boy's actions have an inner, an intellectual importance, that they indicate his mental tendencies and are therefore *symbolical.*"—*E., p. 118.*

Here, again, *significant* would be a better English translation than *symbolical.*

Again, in accordance with his belief in instinct, Froebel declares that it is his "firm conviction that wherever we find anything that gives children ever freshly a joy belonging to real life there is at the bottom of it something important for a child's life." When he sees that children often enjoy going to church and joining in the singing at an age when the words can have no meaning, he says: "All the spontaneous activity of child-life is *symbolical* (Sinnbildlich)." But there is not a word of anything that is ordinarily called "symbolical" in what follows, so far as the child is concerned. The little one is supposed to have "reached a new life-stage," viz. "the dim anticipation that he is not alone in life, but one amid mankind." Consequently he is attracted by "assembly life." The most ardent believer in symbolism can make little of the very practical answers the mother is told to give to the child's questions. He is to be answered "out of the range of his own experience, feelings and ideas, his own intellectual development and necessities." He is to be told that when he is old enough to go to church, he will not only like to hear the organ, but will find out "why flowers bloom and birdies sing and why we still remember Christmas Day."

There is another child in the Mother Songs, who wants to visit the moon, and drags his mother towards the ladder that he may climb up. According to the translator Froebel says he wants to point out "the higher symbolical meaning." But what he says is that one remark presses itself upon him, how "we ought to cultivate intelligently the child's observation of and pleasure in the moon, and in the night sky, and not let this sink into the formlessness and emptiness of mere wonder." For example, it is, he says, quite as easy to tell a child that the moon is a beautiful bright swimming ball, as to say it is a man; or that the stars are sparkling suns which look small because they are far away, as to call them "golden pins," and he adds "Truth never injures, but error always does."

There are certainly some instances in which Froebel found for the tendencies and actions of children, a meaning that does not commend itself to common sense, but as a rule he only "ventures to suggest" rather than insists, and his practical application is generally unobjectionable. We assent willingly, when Froebel tells us that rhythmic movement, passive as well as active, is the earliest beginning of all ordered activity. But we smile when, in accounting for the childish interest in clocks, after allowing for the mystery, he goes on:

"Let me hold the opinion that a deeply slumbering notion of the importance of time lies at the bottom of the pleasure children take in playing with a clock."—*M., p. 139.*

As he truly and naïvely remarks, "this opinion of mine hurts, as an opinion, neither the child nor any one else," and the application may, even in this instance, be useful as he says it is, viz. that we should use this pleasure to instil the beginnings of punctuality or law and order. As an opinion it is not worthy of Froebel's insight, and we can only say that instances of this kind are really negligible, though some have been unnecessarily emphasized by certain Froebelians to whom they appeal.

There are, it is true, a few instances which deserve the strictures which have been heaped up somewhat rashly. It is only put as a question, but Froebel does say of children's pleasure in circle games, "May not their delight spring from the longing and efforts to get an all-round, or all-sided, grasp of an object?"

As to metaphor, Froebel delights in this; his bent of mind is to take pleasure in all analogies, and he suggests that the mother should make more use of the metaphors implied in ordinary language. For example, he speaks of "the transferred moral meaning of such words and phrases as '*straight* and *straightforward*,' and of '*walking in crooked paths*.'" In using little finger plays to give a child control over his hands, the mother is told to think how important for later life is "the right handling of things, in the actual as well as in the figurative sense." The wise mother is represented as cherishing the child's love of light and brightness, saying, "Never shrink away from light"; and while she shows the picture she says, "Here is a boy who has broken the window and now he must go a long way to fetch the glazier unless he can content himself with a dark board that will keep out the dear bright light. You must not heedlessly stop Light's entering your heart and mind, for if you do, you will have to buy it back by trouble and loss of time lest heart and mind become dark. Open your door and little window to the light." Thus she makes the child "see inner things through the outer," and uses his pleasure in light to make him hate deeds of darkness. But there is no harm in all this, the words are used as a clergyman uses the half-dozen words of his text, as a germ of thought which he cultivates, as a finger-post pointing the way in which our minds may travel. And Froebel, like the clergyman, sometimes travels far from the branching of the roads.

Froebel's curious attempts at etymology ought perhaps to be mentioned as a weak point, though they really do not affect his theories, psychological or educational, one way or another. The ball, as the child's first object through which he gains his first perceptions of solidity, weight, mass, etc., is described as on that account "an image of the universe" (der B—all ist der Bild des Alles). The thought is worth having, the pseudo-etymology does not much matter.

To sum up, then, there is mysticism in Froebel's writings as addressed to the adult, and with this no one has any right to quarrel even if it should not appeal to him or her personally. But an undue preponderance has been given to this side of Froebel by those to whom it appeals, or so it seems to me. It does not appeal to me, nor can I perceive that it affects to any appreciable extent the educational theories based on the psychological grounds so carefully considered by Froebel. To writers like Miss Blow, the author of "Symbolic Education," such a statement would no doubt seem outrageous. With intellectual people possessed of Miss Blow's philosophic insight, children may be safe from artificiality and sentimentality. But the average teacher is incapable of philosophy, and when the uncultured mind is supplied with food it cannot digest, that mind is starved. The teacher who glibly uses phrases which she does not understand has reached a state of mind immeasurably below plain ignorance, for it is destructive of honest thought and common sense.[47] The main business of the Froebelian is to forward the cause to which Froebel devoted his life "to bring about a more general use of progressive development in the culture and education of children. We must throw overboard everything that hampers action and set before ourselves, as in his day Froebel tells us he attempted to do, the definite task of "founding anew the practical methods of actual teaching so as to bring them into satisfactory relation with the needs of our life of to-day."

CHAPTER X
Some Criticisms Answered

Professor Adams ends the first chapter of his delightfully witty "Herbartian Psychology" with a challenge to all educational thinkers to come out of their caves and defend their idols. Throughout the book, there is many a side-thrust at Froebel, all of a more or less disparaging nature, in spite of the humorous twinkle which has a fairly permanent abode in the eye of the writer.

Some of the accusations are tolerably sweeping, for example, that Froebelianism "as a psychology is simply non-existent"; that Froebel has failed to correlate theory and practice; that although in "The Education of Man" "we have beautiful, if obscurely expressed, truths about education," yet the Kindergarten cannot be evolved from it, in fact "between the two there is a great gulf fixed, a gulf that Froebel has not bridged."

But the main contention is that Froebel disapproves in theory of any interference with the natural course of development. The Froebelian teacher is thus, according to Professor Adams, reduced to the position of a "humble under-gardener" who merely watches with interest and admiration, and education becomes "a general paralysis."

Mr. Graham Wallas, whose objections to Froebel, or at least to Froebelianism[48], as he understands it, are well known, bases these on the ground that because he was a pre-Darwinian evolutionist, Froebel was bound to overrate the importance of the innate as a factor in development, and to undervalue the other factor of environment.

Professor O'Shea disposes of Froebel in one sentence and in much the same way, as an advocate of what he calls "the doctrine of Unfoldment," where "everything is inner and self-relating," as opposed to the conception gained from Biology, which "implies that the business of a human being is to get properly related to the world—religious, social and physical—of which he is an integral part."

If Froebel really believed that development is entirely from within, as stated by Professor O'Shea, or if he failed to realize the importance of the surroundings, as Mr. Graham Wallas expresses it, he would naturally disapprove of any interference, as Professor Adams says he does. The Froebelian, being thus reduced to passive watching, the mere provision of a Kindergarten would be an interference with the surroundings and a contradiction in practice of the theory of non-interference. If non-interference is really the theory propounded in "The Education of Man," there certainly is a gulf between it and the Kindergarten, a gulf it would be difficult to bridge.

But Froebelians are not prepared to admit the premises of any of these critics. It seems to many of us that these and all similar criticisms are due to misunderstanding. This is sometimes clearly due to careless reading, and consequent want of attention to the context, but even where this is not the case, misunderstandings occur. Few, of late years, have made any real study of Froebel's writings as a whole, such as is necessary to get at his real meaning, which is often obscured by prolixities and repetitions, and sometimes hidden among apparent trivialities.

Professor O'Shea, for example, does not seem to be aware to what extent Froebel, like himself, derived his educational aim and principles from biology. He has probably never realized the deep interest taken by Froebel in the then all-absorbing question of natural development. Clearly he has no idea that Froebel has given expression to a conception of education, practically identical with that given above which he himself draws from biology,[49] and sets in contrast with the one he unjustly attributes to Froebel.

There is no doubt whatever that Froebel laid much stress on what is innate. In his generation, he tells us the child was looked upon "as a piece of wax, or lump of clay, which man can mould into what he pleases." Because Froebel was a student of biology he knew better. He knew, as we have seen, that human beings have instincts, innate tendencies or dispositions differing from those of the lower animals chiefly in their indefiniteness. We are not so afraid of the word "innate" nowadays, when both innate ideas and innate faculties are safely buried, and that Froebel had no dealings with these has been amply shown.

But that this stress on innate tendencies implies that the child is to unfold from within, the educator standing by passive[50], or that Froebel imagined that the developing process could go on with little or no reference to the environment, is quite another matter.

Few of Froebel's critics have taken the trouble to look up the original German before pronouncing condemnation, and this explains part of the injustice that has been done to him. The passage upon which much, perhaps most, of the adverse criticism is based is the one in which Froebel applies to education the term "leidend," translated "passive" in both the English, or, rather, American editions of "The Education of Man." The translation of "leidend" as "passive" is not a happy one. Moreover, the translators have endeavoured to help the reader by dividing the text into numbered sections, a proceeding which though often helpful, sometimes tends to break the continuity of Froebel's thought. This effect is heightened in Hailmann's translation by the interpolated notes, however valuable as some of these are in themselves. This passage, however, opens with "*therefore*," and those who take exception to it ought to have considered the preceding argument. Fair criticism looks back to see why and under what circumstances education is to be "passive or following," as opposed to "dictating and limiting."

In the first place, absolutely passive education is a contradiction in terms. Froebel begins by stating that:

"Education consists in leading man as a thinking, intelligent being, growing into self-consciousness, to a pure, conscious and free representation of the law of his being, and in teaching him ways and means thereto."

He defines the *Theory of Education* as "the system of directions derived from the knowledge and study of that law to guide human beings in the apprehension of their life-work"; and the *Practice of Education* as "the self-active application of this knowledge in the direct development and cultivation of rational beings towards the attainment of their destiny."

To go on from this to say, on the next page but one, that the educator is to do nothing, to stand aside and be truly passive, would be absurd.

That our word "passive" is not the equivalent of Froebel's word "leidend," is easily proved, for in another passage where Froebel does mean "passive" he couples "leidend" with "inactive," and puts passive in a bracket beside it. The passage runs: "wo das Kind äusserlich als unthätig, leidend (passiv) erscheint." In the passage under discussion "passiv" does not appear at all, and "leidend" is coupled, not with "inactive," but with "following," and is contrasted with "dictating, limiting and interfering."[51]

A few lines further we read how the gardener may even destroy the vine "if he fail *in his work* passively and attentively to follow the nature of the plant." He cannot surely "work" and be inactively passive at the same time.

A more correct translation of "leidend" here would perhaps be "tolerant" or "suffering" in its old sense of "permitting," "bearing with," or having patience with.

As to immediate context, Froebel has just stated that education ought "to lift man to a knowledge of himself and mankind, to a knowledge of God and Nature, and to the pure and consecrated life conditioned thereby." "But," he goes on, "education must be founded on what is essential or innermost, and though the real nature of things can only be known by outer manifestations, yet it behoves the educator to be very careful how he judges, for the child that appears good outwardly, is often not really good, i.e. does not will the good from his own determination, or from love, respect for or recognition of it," while "the outwardly rough self-willed child often has within him a vigorous struggle to do what seems to him right." Judging from outer manifestations furnishes constant occasion for false judgments concerning the motives of children, for endless misunderstanding between parent and child, and for unreasonable demands made upon children.

And here comes the force of the conjunction: "*Therefore*," says Froebel, "education, instruction and training in their fundamental principles must necessarily be tolerant, following, not dictating, not limiting or defining, not interfering."

What is it, then, that Froebel is telling us to follow almost passively, interfering, in our ignorance, as little as possible? Simply the natural order of development, the natural instincts of childhood, which in this very passage he is arguing are as trustworthy as those of other young animals. Here, as everywhere, man can only control Nature *by following*, by obeying her laws.

"As the duckling hastens to the pond and the chicken scratches the ground, so will the human being, still young, still, as it were, in the process of creation, though as unconsciously as any Nature product, yet definitely and surely desire what is best for him. We give plants and animals time and space and freedom to develop, but the young human being is to man a piece of wax, a lump of clay, from which he can mould what he will. O man, who roamest through garden and field, through meadow and grove, why dost thou close thy mind to the silent teaching of Nature?"—*E., p. 8.*

Surely we have here a plea to "suffer (leiden) little children," to bear with the little one, still, as Froebel describes him, "still, as it were, in the process of creation," nay, more, a plea for the actual recognition and fostering of these instinctive tendencies which Professor Dewey calls "the foundation-stones of educational method," rather than a recommendation to "gratify every youthful impulse," or to stand aside altogether. For the context, the whole, is not yet complete.

Froebel goes on to say that if we are certain of any tendency to unhealthy development we are to interfere with full severity (so tritt geradezubestimmende, fordernde Erziehungsweise in ihrer ganzen Strenge ein).

And now comes a sentence apparently quite overlooked by Mr. Graham Wallas, who blames Froebel for underestimating the environment. In the mean-time, until we are sure that our interference is justifiable, "nothing is left for us to do but to bring the child into relations and surroundings in all respects adapted to him."[52]—*E., p. 11.*

In many other passages Froebel shows plainly that he had no thought of the "gratifying of every youthful impulse" in the sense of individual caprice.

In his plea for monetary help to establish Kindergartens and training establishments connected with them, he complains that in existing institutions children are either "repressed and their energies crippled, *or else we are confronted with the wild and uncontrollable character which results when children are uncared for and are left altogether to their own impulses."—L., p. 159.*

"Life has no room for wilfulness and whims," he says in his Mother Songs; "Boyhood is the age of Discipline" he states in "The Education of Man." But, as he himself sums up this discussion:

"All true education is double-sided, prescribing and following, active and passive, positive yet giving scope, firm and yielding.... Between educator and pupil should rule invisibly a third something to which both are equally subject. The third something is the right, the best ... the child, the pupil has a very keen apprehension whether what father or teacher requests is personal and arbitrary or the expression of general law and necessity."—*E., p. 14.*

The proof of whether or not the educator has succeeded in rightly adjusting the claims of freedom and authority, Froebel expresses in words recalling Kant's, "When the 'Thou Shalt' of the Law becomes the 'I will' of the doer, then we are free."

"In good education, in genuine instruction, in true teaching, necessity must and will call forth freedom, law will call forth self-determination, and outer compulsion inner free-will.

"Where necessity produces bondage, where law brings fraud and crime, and outer compulsion causes slavery, there every effect of education is destroyed. There oppression destroys and debases, severity and harshness bring obstinacy and deceit, and the burden is more than can be borne."—*E., p. 14.*

To emphasize the fact that Froebel did realize the importance of environment, and to anticipate the criticism that this shortened rendering is an interpretation in the light of modern educational theories, of Froebel's somewhat cumbrous phrases, we can turn to a passage in his later writing, part of which has been quoted elsewhere:

"Through the child's efforts to repel that which is contrary to the needs of his life, indignation and discontent are awakened; and on the other hand, from the fact that his normal desires are ungratified, they become inordinate and mischievous. How may parents avoid these evil results? Most satisfactorily through a threefold yet single glance at life. Let them look into themselves, and their own course of development and its requirements, let them recall their own earliest years, then later stages of development, and look deeply into their present life. Next, let them look equally deeply into the life of the child and what he must require for his present stage of development. Having scrutinized what the child needs, *let them scrutinize his environment,* and first observe what it offers and does not offer for the fulfilment of such requirements. Let them utilize all offered possibilities of meeting normal needs; and when such needs cannot be met, let them recognize this fact, and show the child plainly the impossibility of their fulfilment. Finally, let them clearly recognize whatever *in the child's environment* tends to awaken antagonism and discontent, remove it if it be removable, and admit its defect if it be not removable."[53]—*P., p. 167.*

It is, of course, true that Froebel was pre-Darwinian in time, but it is equally true that he was post-Darwinian in many of his beliefs.

To find out whether or not his educational doctrines are really based on false or exploded theories of development, as the Criticism of Mr. Graham Wallas implies, we must gather together from Froebel's various writings, his most important references to the subject.

The key-note to his interest in it lies probably in the yearning for unity and union in all relations, which was a part of his individuality. This may have dated back to the time when, a puzzled little mortal of eight or nine years old, he was most unwisely allowed to hear his father exhorting and rebuking his parishioners. It seemed to the boy that most of the trouble arose from the fact that human beings, and human beings alone, so far as he knew, were divided into two sexes, and he felt that he would have arranged matters differently. Comfort came to him when his older brother, by showing him the male and female flower of the hazel, gave him some idea of a great law of Nature. Strange comfort, too, it seems, for a boy not yet ten years old!

The late Mr. Ebenezer Cooke pointed out long ago[54] that Mr. Graham Wallas had not only overshot the mark in saying that "Darwin transferred the cause of development from within to without," but that he had himself failed to draw any distinction between the facts of development, as seen in the individual, and the theory of the origin or development of species, which we associate with the names of Darwin and Wallace. Mr. Cooke pointed to Froebel's connection with Batch, the founder of a Natural History Society, of which Goethe was a member, as showing that he was in direct touch with those who were working out the theory of development of the individual.

Froebel himself refers to this Natural History Society in his Autobiography, saying that "students," of whom he was one, "who had shown living interest and done active work in Natural Science," were invited to become members, and that this awoke within him "a yearning towards higher scientific knowledge." At this time Froebel was but a youth of seventeen, with no idea that education was to be his life work. Three years later, he meets a private tutor, "a young man quite out of the common, with actively inquiring mind," who was "especially fond of making comprehensive schemes of education." The year after this we find him reading what he can of anthropology and history, and saying of his reading: "It taught me of man in his broad historical relations and set before me the general life of my kind as one great whole."

One year more, and while he is looking for a situation with an architect—in spite of uneasy communing with himself as to how architecture was to be used "for the culture and ennoblement of mankind"—Grüner claps him on the shoulder with "Give up architecture, it is not your vocation at all! Become a teacher."

It is perhaps because Froebel passed thus from interest in biology to interest in education that at this time he gives to his own question, What is the purpose of education?—almost the identical answer that Professor O'Shea puts into the mouth of his biologist[55], and which he sets in opposition to Froebel's supposed opinions:

"In answering the question, What is the purpose of education? I relied at that time on the following observations: Man lives in a world of objects, which influence him and which he desires to influence; therefore he ought to know these objects in their nature, in their conditions and in their relations with each other and with mankind.... I sought, to the extent of such powers as I consciously possessed at that time, to make clear to myself the meaning of all things through man, his relations with himself, and with the external world ... it seemed to me that everything which should or could be required for human education must be necessarily conditioned and given, by virtue of the very nature of the necessary course of his development, in man's own being and in the relations amidst which he is set. A man, it seemed to me, would be well educated when he had been trained to care for these relationships and to acknowledge them, to master them and to survey them."—*A., p. 69.*

In the very beginning, then, of his educational career, Froebel emphasized rather than overlooked "the relationships amidst which man is set," but he was to learn more yet about development.

Six years later he is back at a university, and "just at this time," he says, "those great discoveries of the French and English philosophers became generally known through which the great manifold external world was seen to form a comprehensive outer world."

The English writer may have been Erasmus Darwin. The French writer was no doubt Lamarck, to whom belongs "the immortal glory of having for the first time worked out the theory of Descent as an independent scientific theory of the first order and as the philosophical foundation of the whole science of Biology."

From some such source, at any rate, Froebel must have gained "the key-note of development," viz., that it is always from the undifferentiated to the differentiated. We have already seen that he applied this to mental development and so gained his modern conception of the earliest infant consciousness, "an undifferentiated unorganized unity."

In "The Education of Man" he speaks of

"the all-pervading law of Nature according to which the general gives rise to the particular,"—*E., p. 167.*

and in the Mother Songs he says:

"Whether we are looking at a seed or an egg, whether we are watching feeling or thought, what is definite proceeds everywhere from what is indefinite."—*M., p. 121.*

Or, again:

"In the child as in the grain of seed, there begins a development proceeding towards complexity."—*P., p. 172.*

Such quotations fully exonerate Froebel from belief in any "pre-formation" theory, whether physical or mental, as indeed Mr. Cooke made abundantly plain.

It is in one of his later papers[56] that Froebel generalizes and states very plainly how everything is developed under the influence of its environment.

"Taking Nature as our guide, let us endeavour to find the essential nature of material objects and the conditions under which this develops, for the process of development shows the essence of the developing object.

"*Firstly*, each thing and each object manifesting existence and life, develops itself in accordance with the highest and simplest, the general laws of life. Thus everything manifests these laws and their primeval cause.

"*Secondly*, each thing and each object in Nature develops itself according to its own individuality and the laws of its being.

"*Thirdly*, everything in Nature develops itself under the collective influence of all things. If any object seems to be withdrawn from this collective influence, such withdrawal is only mediate....

"In Nature, and in everything, all things develop as members of the world-whole, the universal life, as members of a whole, each perfect in its kind, because each, while standing in the centre of the collective influence streaming upwards and inwards—nay, in a certain sense, as the receiver, yielding itself to this influence—yet also acts (as assimilative and formative) and develops itself, faithful to the indwelling laws of life universal and particular. We must see clearly the conditions of perfect development in Nature, and then employ them in human life. Thus only can we help man to attain, upon the plane of human development—which means spiritual development—a degree of perfection corresponding to that which the forms and types of Nature show upon the plane of physical development."—*P., p. 196.*

When child development is in question, far from minimising, as he is supposed to do, the importance of environment, parents and teachers are told:

"We must hold fast for consideration in life this fact, that in the spontaneous occupation and playing of the child, not the germ only, but the growing point of his life also, is formed *in union with his surroundings, and under their silent unremarked influence* (im Vereine mit der Umgebung und unter deren stillen unbemerkten Einwirkung)."—*P., p. 108.*

Or, again:

"As the new-born child, like a ripe grain of seed dropped from the mother plant has life in itself, and as it spontaneously develops life *in progressive connection with the common life whole*; so activity and action are the first phenomena of his awakening life. This activity bears the impress of what is innermost, it is an inner activity whose purpose is manifestation of the inner through the outer, and, as leading up to this, devoted to consideration of and working with the outer to penetrating the outer and overcoming hindrances as such."—*P., p. 23.*

This account surely makes plain, that whatever Froebel may have believed with regard to the origin of species, he in no way believed that development in general was a one-sided process, in which the environment went for nothing.

In his "Criticism," Mr. Graham Wallas remarked: "Whoever divorced his educational system from his philosophy, would have seemed to Froebel to have taken all force and meaning out of his work." This is most true, and it approaches absurdity to attribute so limited a view to a man imbued as Froebel was with the philosophical doctrine of the reconciliation of the opposites. [57] That all development was the result of a harmony between opposites was one of his cardinal doctrines.

"We are living in an age," he writes, "when we are consciously under a law of development acting by the reconciliation of opposites."

Mr. Hailmann gives a long footnote where Froebel is quoted as comparing his idea of the law of connection or unification with the ideas of Fichte and Hegel, and saying:

"It is both of these, and yet has nothing in common with either of them; it is the law which the contemplation of Nature has taught me.... And where do we find absolute contrasts that have not somewhere and somehow a connection? In action and reaction the contrasts that we see everywhere give rise to the motions in the universe as they do in the smallest organism. This implies for all development a struggle which however sooner or later will find its adjustment; and this adjustment is the connection of contrasts."—*E., p. 42.*

What Froebel knew of Hegel's philosophy was probably gained from discussions among his friends, for in the hearing of Madame von Marenholz, he said, "I do not know how Hegel formulates and applies this law, for I have had no time for the study of his system," and he went on to say of "the philosophical systems of others" that "most of them belong to a theory of the world that is passing away, whose one-sidedness becomes more apparent every day" (Reminiscences, 225). Ebers, too, speaks of Froebel's ideas as opposed to those of Hegel.

Even Mr. Graham Wallas allows that Froebel's casual references to the development of species are "surprisingly modern." No orthodox views as to the exact date of the creation of the world keep him from accepting the newly discovered testimony of the rocks as to "the remains of perished ages." Ardent as his religious convictions were, they had a philosophic width unusual indeed in his day. The Garden of Eden is to him a parable, repeated "in the experience of every child from the time of his appearance on earth to the time when he consciously (by the help of names) beholds himself in beautiful Nature spread out before him." In each child he sees "repeated at a later period, the deed which marks the beginning of moral and human emancipation, of the dawn of reason."

He refers calmly to

"the fall, or, since the result is the same, the ascent of the mind of man, from simple, uniform, emotional development, into the development of externally analytic and critical reason."—*E., p. 194.*

Not Stanley Hall himself insists more that the development of the individual shall follow the development of the race, and this in 1826, two years before Baer, and four years before Comte, to whom Herbert Spencer attributed the doctrine. "Humanity," he says, "lives only in its continuous development."

"Each successive generation and each successive individual human being, inasmuch as he would understand the past and present, must pass through all preceding phases of human development and culture, and this should not be done in the way of dead imitation or mere copying, but in the way of living spontaneous self-activity."—*E., p. 18.*

There is certainly no ground for assuming that Froebel held any such pre-Darwinian views as a special creation of each species, for there is no point on which he insists more emphatically than that in Nature development is continuously progressive.

"In God's world, just because it is God's world, by Him created, one thing constant is expressed to which we give the name of unbroken progression of development in all and through all."[58]—*M., p. 154.*

"God neither ingrafts nor inoculates, He develops the most trivial and imperfect things in continuously ascending series and in accordance with eternal self-grounded and self-developing laws."—*E., p. 328.*

Mr. Winch makes merry over Froebel's sentence:

"As Man and Nature have one origin, they must be subject to the same laws,"

and remarks that "this conception is almost completely given up…. Our view now rather is one in which God and Nature are at strife, in which the ethical interest overcomes Nature…."

But Froebel is far ahead of this. The great law to him is the Law of Development to which Man and Nature, which includes Man, are subject. The ethical interest is not, as Mr. Winch intimates, something transcending Nature, but is itself evolved. Morality, Froebel distinctly tells us, is "rooted" in Instinct, and "human development means spiritual development."

Professor O'Shea says of the doctrine of Unfoldment which he attributes to Froebel that it "regards man on his spiritual side as an entity set apart from everything in the universe."[59]

Froebel, however, writes:

"Difficult, very difficult, would it be to define where the purely physical ends and the purely intellectual begins. It is precisely on account of this close welding or flowing into one another of the Physical and Psychical, the bodily and mental, the material and spiritual, the vital (des Vitalen) and intellectual, instinct and morality; it is because of this rooting of the higher in the lower that the training and ennobling of the senses, such as smell and taste, are so important."—*M., p. 183.*

"Training and ennobling," these words bring us back to the educational doctrines Froebel based upon what he knew of development, physical and mental, from whatever source he may have gained his information.

"From the beginning of the Darwinian reconstruction of the moral sciences," says Mr. Graham Wallas, "it was absurd, while speaking of 'environment,' to ignore the fact that the deliberate care and contrivance of the parent must form a large part of the environment of the child." Undoubtedly.

But it was because Froebel exalted "the deliberate care and contrivance of the parent" that he wrote "The Education of Man," to tell his generation how best to care and contrive. It was because he realized that this deliberate care and contrivance must begin from the very first that he wrote his Mother Songs. He tells the mother here that "if she is wise, in all she does a noble meaning lies"; that she must "do nothing aimlessly or she'll create a child she cannot educate." He tells her that it is "by watching what makes the child's eyes bright, that she will know how best to give delight," and that she must "seek to strengthen power and mind in all things."

In very truth the Kindergarten itself, with all its imperfections, is nothing more nor less than an attempt to supply that very environment which its founder is supposed to undervalue—an attempt to foster, by providing suitable conditions, those innate tendencies or natural activities, to which Froebel attached infinite importance.

This is why the discovery of the name Kindergarten gave Froebel the pleasure expressed in his cry, "Eureka, I have it! Kindergarten shall be its name." The original designation contained the actual words "through the culture of the instinct for activity, inquiry and creation, inherent in man," but this original title spreads over several lines of print. "Garden" to Froebel expresses just what he wanted, "As in a garden under God's favour, and *by the care of a skilled, intelligent gardener*, growing plants are cultivated in accordance with Nature's laws, so here, in our child-garden, shall the noblest of all growing things, *men* (that is, children, the germs and shoots of humanity), be cultivated in accordance with the laws of their own being, of God and of Nature."—*L., p. 161.*

This is why he urges on his pupil, Ida Seele, to retain the name in spite of the prejudices it aroused. It is to her that he writes:

"Is there really such importance underlying the mere name of a system?—some one might ask. Yes, there is: … It is true that any one carefully watching your teaching would observe a new spirit … you would strike him as personally capable, nay, as extremely capable, but you would fail to strike him as priestess of the idea, and of the struggle towards the realization of the idea—education by development—the destined means of raising the whole human race. For, after all, what do we mean by 'Kindergarten'?… No man can acquire fresh knowledge beyond the measure which his own mental strength and stage of development fits him to receive. But little children have no development at all.… Infant schools are nothing but a contradiction of child nature. Little children ought not to be *schooled* and taught, they merely need to be developed. It is the pressing need of our age, and only the idea of a garden can serve to show us symbolically the proper treatment of children. This idea lies in the very name of a Kindergarten. … How much better had you been able to call your work by its proper name, and to make evident by that expression, the real nature of the new spirit you have introduced."—*L., p. 290.*

There is no gulf between the Kindergarten, and "The Education of Man," with its appeal to educators to follow instead of interfering with Nature's methods, to foster instead of repressing the "instincts of activity and of construction," to foster play, which though "merely natural life," yet holds "the seed leaves of all later life."

Froebel's gardener is "skilled and intelligent," and a skilled gardener is supposed to have scientific knowledge of his plants, of the conditions of soil, exposure, etc., best suited to them. Professor Adams says that "to call a child a plant does not advance matters much, and it certainly does not account for the use of the cubes, spheres and such like." This, however, it does most certainly if these cubes and spheres are the right food material for the child's mind, as Froebel at any rate believed.

All the employments of the Kindergarten, all the varied materials, the sand and clay, the pencil and paint brush, the building blocks, cardboard, sawdust, moss, nut-shells, etc., for constructive or "representative" play are definitely mentioned and definitely commended in "The Education of Man." They are commended because they are the employments and the material which children everywhere find for themselves; because Froebel had sufficient knowledge of biology to know that instinctive action must somehow benefit the individual and the race; and also because he had psychological insight enough to see that by such activities children gain not merely skill, but clear ideas and "firmness of will."

Professor Adams writes: "Not Philosophy, but common sense, experience and loving observation, have led Froebel and his followers to adopt certain apparatus and certain methods, which are excellent in themselves, and which in capable hands produce admirable results. For this he deserves all the honour that has been heaped upon him—but he has not explained John."

True enough, Froebel has not explained, at least, he has not entirely explained that charming John, the Professor's own creation and type of all our children. Who has? Still, by his efforts as a pioneer in genetic psychology—the result of his belief that "only by the study of development in ourselves and others, can we learn to understand the child"—and by the two sketches so full of insight into child-life and into boy life, which he has given us in "The Education of Man," surely Froebel has done at least his share even in explaining John.

No doubt he learnt much from "loving observation." Nor does he undervalue it, but, in his case, the observation was induced by the Philosophy, as well as by the love. For, as he tells us, "it is a necessary part of me to be irresistibly driven to search out the ultimate cause of every fact in life, to discover its roots." He learned much from watching both mothers and children, but he says:

"What natural mother wit and human common sense left to themselves, have been doing by chance and piece-meal, ought now to be brought forward by a thoughtful mind, its foundation, connections and deeper meaning recognized, that it may be improved upon by clever and kindly thought."—M., p. 147.

An education which "follows" needs shown by the child, which "follows" the laws of development, physical and mental, as far as these can be discovered from history, from introspection, and from observation of children in general and of "each individual child," that is the "patiently following" education which Froebel puts before us as an ideal. "For," he says:

"By the full application of the latter method of education, the prescribing and interfering, we should wholly lose the sure, steady and progressive development of mankind, which is the ultimate aim and object of all education."—E., p. 10.

Note.—The foregoing chapter was written some years ago, but in 1912 there appeared a fresh criticism of Froebel and his work in many ways more adequate than certain others. It appeared as an Introduction to a new translation of "The Education of Man" and of some of Froebel's lesser writings, by Dr. Fletcher and Professor Welton. In this introduction, important points are granted, for example, that Froebel had "grasped the vital principle that all true development, and consequently all true education, is a self-directed process—that purpose is the key-note of human culture and advance. It was the emphasis which he laid upon this which makes Froebel one of the princes of education and gives him an enduring place in the history of thought." Or again, that Froebel's teaching is "not the negation of all human constraint," but that he sees clearly that "constraint is necessary to train the will to resist impulse and follow purpose"; that with Froebel "Discipline must direct instinctive impulse, not simply oppose and thwart it." Unfortunately, however, the writers of the book do not seem to have grasped the idea of the Kindergarten as an Institution which had this very end in view, and the second part of the book which is called "The Kindergarten," never mentions its essential features. So we have the familiar statement that between the Kindergarten and "The Education of Man" a gulf is fixed, a statement which has been already discussed. And we are also told that Froebel attracts us "by his very vagueness." But Keilhau and Helba and the real Kindergarten are none of them vague. That Froebel attributed too much importance to his Gifts and occupations most of us will readily allow, but that the forms of expression set forth in the Helba plan are to be regarded as merely additions to the Gifts is impossible seeing that the plan for Helba is dated 1829. Besides, all such work had already been very much in evidence at Keilhau (See *p. v*, Preface), and the Gifts and Occupations were an attempt to provide in a similar manner for children very much younger, and as materials are only such as children find for themselves. We claim that Froebel himself is the best interpreter of his own invention, the Kindergarten, and we are content to abide by his own definition of it: *An Institution for the cultivation of the life of mankind through fostering the impulse to activity, investigation and construction in the child; an institution for the self-instruction, for self-education of mankind through play, that is creative self-activity and spontaneous self-instruction.*

APPENDIX I
On the Meaning of the Word "Activity"

Professor Stout is particularly definite in his use of the word "activity," and as he agrees with Mr. Bradley, from whom he quotes "that the current use of the word activity in the literature of philosophy is a scandal," it may be well to inquire here whether Froebel used the word loosely or with some degree of definiteness.

Professor Stout considers the word "activity" specially appropriate to cases "in which the return of a causal process upon itself is especially prominent or important." He quotes from Mr. Bradley again that "Activity seems to be self-caused change. A transition that begins with, and comes out of the thing itself is the process where we feel that it is active." "Thus," Mr. Stout comments, "the life and growth of organisms are specially appropriate examples of activity; for such processes are in a large measure immanent or self-determining."

The first point that suggests itself is that in the majority of cases, Froebel may perhaps be said to have avoided the difficulty by his constant reference not only to activity but to "self-activity," a word associated with the name of Froebel closely as his very shadow.

In the second place, we do find Froebel very markedly referring to the self-determining activity of organisms, in a passage where he is trying to show that all instruction should start from the child's own desire and power of will. He says that the mother—grounding her instruction in her child's desire to write to the absent father—acts like the sun, "whose warmth awakens in every grain of seed, life, impulse, power, self-activity, self-determination" (die Triebe, die Kraft, die Selbstthätigkeit und Selbstbestimmung).[60]

It is Froebel's peculiarity that he brings his philosophical conceptions into the veriest details, and so even in speaking of how the mother may make a ball represent a springing kitten, etc., and saying that to the child the ball is "the uniting object," yet, he says, considering the plays as proceeding from the child (vom Kinde aus), "all activity, though mediated (vermittelt) by the ball, proceeds definitely from the child, and though going through the ball, refers back again to the child, who is himself a unit."

There is a particular passage which suggests that there existed a special definite idea in Froebel's mind in regard to the word "activity," and it is one which presents a difficulty to an ordinary and unphilosophical mind, though a possible light is thrown upon it by Mr. Bradley's definition. In this passage activity (Thätigkeit) is very distinctly given as something higher than impulse (Triebe).

The working of the primeval Cause, "the uniting," is called, Froebel says, "according to the different stages in development, Force, Impulse, Life, Life-impulse, Activity" (Wirken, Trieb, Leben, Lebenstrieb, Thätigkeit).

This placing of activity so high in the scale is at least no accident, and conscious self-determination is constantly attributed to man as "the most perfect earthly being," and to man alone.

Mr. Stout proceeds to examine the conception of self-determining process, with special reference to changes within the sphere of an individual consciousness, taking as the most convenient point of departure, such illustrative analogies as come from the physical world, and beginning with the simplest form of self-determination, the law of inertia.[61]

"Conscious life," he says, "is always in some degree self-sustaining, this indeed is an indispensable part of the connotation of all such words as activity, endeavour, conation, effort, striving, will, attention. All such terms imply that the process to which they refer, tends by its intrinsic nature in a certain direction, or toward a certain end."

Now the word "endeavour" or "effort" (Streben) is a word Froebel constantly uses in speaking of a child's activity, and he does more than merely "imply" that this process "tends in a certain direction, or toward a certain end" when he affirms that "In every activity, in every deed of man, and of the smallest child, an aim is expressed."

Professor Stout goes on to say that in conscious states we can always distinguish between determination from within and from without, and "it is a point of vital significance that this distinction coincides with that between mental activity and mental passivity."[62] With mental passivity Froebel has but few dealings, if indeed he has any. There is one passage in which he uses the word passive (passiv); this, however, merely states that the child, in accommodating himself to his surroundings, may outwardly appear inactive or passive, but only in order to have more scope for his inner activity (wo es äusserlich als unthätig, leidend [passiv] erscheint … um so seiner innern Thätigkeit mehr Spielraum zu verschaffen).

From what he does say there is little doubt but that Froebel would willingly have subscribed to Professor Stout's dictum, "that to be mentally active is identical with being mentally alive or awake,[63] though in degree the activity may shade off gradually from that "involving a sense of strain, to that of almost passivity." But just as Professor Stout rejects the idea of purely passive consciousness, so, too, does he reject "pure" mental activity. "It is impossible to find any bit of mental process which is determined purely from within."[64]… "At the same time it is equally true that no change within is entirely determined from without."[65] Mr. Stout does not say that pure activity—a purely self-determined process—cannot exist, for "we should, by parity of reasoning, be bound to reject the second law of motion."[66] "But it rests," he says, "with the advocates of pure activity, if there are such, to adduce a case of it, and until such a case is brought forward we must assume that there is none.… No portion of matter can be, even for a moment, outside the sphere of influence of other portions."

We have seen that Mr. O'Shea practically accuses Froebel of being an "advocate of pure activity,"[67] nor is he the only one of Froebel's critics who does so. If, however, it be considered an accident that Froebel should in one passage put "conscious self-determination" at the highest point of life development, and in another passage give this place to "activity" which Mr. Bradley and Mr. Stout tell us is to be regarded as self-determined, is it also an accident that in the very same passage Froebel should state that "everything in Nature develops and forms itself under the total collective influence of all other things"?

If these correspondences are not accidental, then it must be allowed in the first place that Froebel attached a fairly definite meaning to the word "activity," including self-determination in its connotation; and in the second place that the grounds on which he is charged with being a believer in "pure activity" are very insufficient. When Mr. Stout says that even if it is allowable "as an illustrative hypothesis" to regard the physical universe as an internally complete system, [68] it is clear that "the stream of individual consciousness is no such self-contained unit," but "the merest fragment of universal reality, as its correlated brain process is the merest fragment of the material world[69]"; is this anything but a statement of that unity, on which Froebel insists in season and out of season—which appears on almost every page of his writings, so that the word has become the veriest "cant" of the half-trained Kindergarten teacher[70].

The philosophic conception of unity, the belief that there is no separation in either world, physical or psychical, or between either world, was always present to Froebel's mind. "In Nature," he writes, "every phenomenon has its sufficient foundation and its necessary consequence." But as every philosopher would say, so Froebel said, "Separation is permitted for the observing, thinking and comparing intellect, and the outwardly representing life, and is indeed required by it, but must by no means on that account be permitted to appear in the mind which is intended to grasp and constantly to retain in its original inner union, that which is outwardly apparently separated by the thinking intellect, the reason and the life."[71] So Professor Münsterberg, writing as a professed scientist, says, "Science is to me, not a mass of disconnected information, … but the certainty that nothing can exist outside the gigantic mechanism of causes and effects, but Science is not and cannot be, and ought never to try to be, an expression of ultimate reality."[72]

It would never have dawned on Froebel, nor would it have appealed to him, to separate his philosophy from his science, but there is no more contradiction in Froebel's "self-activity" which is influenced from without, than there is in Professor Stout when he speaks of self-determination as included in the connotation of "activity," and adds that until a case of "pure activity" is brought forward, we must assume that there is none.

Of all his "means of play," Froebel says:

"In order, therefore, on the one hand to introduce the child to the handling of his play material, we gave him the ball, … but each of these means of play summons the child in return to self-activity, to free self-activity; to movement, to free independent movement" (zur Selbsthätigkeit, zur freien Selbsthätigkeit; zur Bewegung, zur freien, inabhängigen Bewegung). [73]

APPENDIX II
Comparison of Plays noted by Froebel with the Enumeration given by Groos

Much that is given in Groos' more elaborate classification can also be found in Froebel's suggestions, particularly where younger children are concerned. For plays coming under the heading of Playful Activity of the Sensory Apparatus, Froebel has a parallel for every kind except that of Temperature, and for this Groos has not himself found anything that can fairly be called play.

For Sensations of Contact there is the Kicking Play, and Taste and Smell are also represented in the Mother Play book. For Hearing play we have the wooden ball, "a plaything for the child liable to produce noise by its movement," as well as the Tic-tac and Finger Piano plays, and for receptive play, the mother is told to speak, rhythmically if possible, or to sing with every play. For Sensations of Brightness we have "Mother you want to foster this delight in all things that are sparkling clear and bright" of the "Fish in the Brook," as well as "The Lightbird," which Froebel has "found over and over again in all grades of the culture that makes up social life in village and in town."

Sensations of colour are well provided for. In "The Two Windows" we have: "See the beautiful coloured circles and rays, just like rainbow and dew-drops, see how beautifully the colours play through each other." Colour is a feature in Gift I, in beadwork, in the tablets, in paper folding, cutting and plaiting, and besides these there are crayons and paints, and frequent reference is made to the child's pleasure in the colour of flowers.

Froebel also makes much play depend on perception of form: "Attention to the form and figure of the object can also be utilized for the child in play," or, again, "Early in life the child delights in round and varied pebbles, he seeks and collects them, he takes pleasure in the straight edged and right angled." He has found "The Target" play very widely spread, "plainly because it contains, as I see it, the first trace of an endeavour to make a child notice position and form."

For perception of movement, to which Froebel would have added perception of change of position, there are many plays with the ball as well as "Tic-tac," "The Child and the Pigeons," "The Lightbird," "The Fish in the Brook," etc.

Groos' next class is Play with the Motor Apparatus and under this comes first Playful movement of the Bodily Organs. Here we have Froebel saying: "The first toys and occupations of the child come from himself: he plays with his own limbs."—*L., p. 108.* "The child at this stage begins to play with his limbs—his hands, his fingers, his lips, his tongue, his feet, as well as with the expression of his eyes and face."—*E., p. 48.*

Under playful locomotion, Groos actually quotes Froebel's description of the child learning to walk, and we have also marching, running, and racing games; "the large majority," says Froebel, "I have created simply by watching the children at play.... Thus I have prepared a limping-game because I see my boys always limping and hopping."

Next comes Playful Movement of Foreign Bodies, and under this heading Groos gives "Hustling things about, pushing, pulling, shaking, seizing and pushing away, dabbling in water, handling sand and clay, kite-flying, and capture of insects." Of these Froebel mentions pushing of carriages, kite-flying, hobby-horse riding; he makes much of play with water, sand and clay, and he speaks of the catching of insects, etc., desiring that it should be wisely checked by directing the activity into other channels.

As to Destructive or Analytic Movement Play, Froebel notes that: "The child wishes to know all the properties of the thing, for this reason he examines it on all sides; for this reason he tears and breaks it; for this reason he puts it in his mouth and bites it."—*E., p. 73.* "The cruel treatment of insects and other animals originates in the little boy's desire to obtain an insight into the life of the animal."—*E., p. 164.*

Of Constructive or Synthetic Movement Play, so much has been said already, that it is not necessary to dwell on it. Froebel, in fact, gives a far more inclusive account of this than Groos himself, not omitting his "simplest form," viz. moulding new forms with sand, etc., nor the collecting and arranging in rows which to Groos and to Froebel is a more primitive form of construction. Of Exercise of Endurance, too, we have spoken, in quoting passages where Froebel shows the boyish desire to measure and to increase strength. Throwing and Catching Plays have their place in the "Apprentice and Master Workman" game.

The important third class, the Playful Use of the Higher Mental Powers, includes according to Groos a good deal that he has dealt with under other heads, e.g. Memory Play includes (*a*) Recognition and (*b*) Reflective Memory. Under the former comes that pleasure in recognition of form which has already been dealt with, the pleasure given by pictures, often, says Groos, greater than is given by the reality. Froebel, too, says that if the father makes a sketch, "this man of lines, this horse of lines, will give the child more joy than an actual man, an actual horse will do."—*E., p. 77.* Froebel, too, notes the pleasure it will give a child to name flowers through recognition of a form: "Spurred like a rider, circled like a snail, umbrellas, wheels, he'll find the names."—*M., p. 181.* There is also the recognition of animal and other noises, as in Froebel's Yard Gate. Rote learning as a play Froebel hardly mentions.

As to the two groups which Groos brings under the heading of Imagination, viz. "Illusion either playful or serious," and "the voluntary or involuntary transformation of our mental content," these receive full recognition. Froebel notes how the stick becomes a horse or the knotted handkerchief the baby, as well as the play of listening to and inventing stories.

Under the head of Attention comes such games as Hide and Seek, because of the alternate stress and relaxation, and Froebel noted before Darwin did the pleasure of the baby in Bo-peep. Groos also brings curiosity under this heading, and we have seen that Froebel deals fully with such play as the outcome of the instinct of investigation, or the instinct for self-teaching.

Froebel would certainly not draw the line where Groos does, when he says "the true characteristics of play are in inverse ratio to the intensity of the desire for knowledge," and if this rule were strictly adhered to, a good deal of what Groos does call play might have to come out.

The plays which fall under the head of Reason have two bearings, says Groos, first causality, and second inherence. There are various references to the "joy of being a cause" from the child "whose capacity for speech is as yet undeveloped," but who draws away the support and as the cube falls "turns to his mother in joyous triumph," up to the pride of Keilhau boys, who "might not have accomplished their fortresses without the sapper," but "who believed that if cast on a desert island, each could build a hut of his own." Froebel also brings in intellectual games such as draughts, and he notes how children will invent their own words and their own alphabets in play. Of the making and solving of riddles I think Froebel never speaks.

As to what Groos says of Experimentation with the feelings, the parallels in Froebel are surprise plays such as Hide and Seek, adventure and hunting games where there may be play with fear, and the legends and stories.

Under the Impulse of the Second or Socionomic order, come the Fighting Plays, Love Play, Imitative Play, and Social Play. Of Love Play, Froebel has none, but the hunting and fighting were allowed abundant scope at Keilhau. Of Imitative Play there is much that can be cited from the playful imitation of simple movements and sounds in the Mother Songs and the Kindergarten Games, to the "classic dramas" of the Keilhau boys. Plastic and constructive play, too, goes from the simplest sand play, through the Kindergarten handwork, not only up to the fortress making, but also to the "boxes with locks and hinges, so neatly finished, veneered, and polished that many a trained cabinet-maker's apprentice could have done no better," which were made at Keilhau.

Of the Social Plays Groos says with feeling that, however advisable, it is wellnigh impossible to make a distinct class. He starts, however, with the "need of bodily association or the herding instinct." He brings in the child's eager desire to be with his fellows, and the importance in adult life of festivals, religious or otherwise. He mentions the child's voluntary submission to a leader, and speaks of play as instrumental in teaching children submission to law. We have noticed Froebel speaking of the "combined games, which will train the child, by his very nature eager for companionship, in the habit of association with comrades, in good fellowship and all that this implies." He also wants the child to take alternately some special part in the game and to be merely one of the crowd: "Each child should have a chance to lead, for it is especially developing to a child to recognize himself as independent as well as a member of the whole." Among the older boys, the Bergwachts for instance were carefully organized under separate leaders and the captain of the first band was director of the whole. Froebel, too, made much of festivals at Keilhau, and this has always been a recognized feature of the Kindergarten.

Enjoyment of the comic never, I think, makes its appearance at all. Froebel had many gifts, but the saving sense of humour does not appear to have been among them.

FOOTNOTES

[1] See Chapter IX.

[2] See Chapter X.

[3] "Froebel's Educational Principles," Elementary School Record, Vol. I, No. 5, or "The Dewey School," published by the Froebel Society.

[4] See Chapter VI, *p. 79.*

[5] The Philosophy and Psychology of the Kindergarten.—"Teachers' College Record," Nov., 1903.

[6] It is true that Froebel was pre-Darwinian, but see *p. 198.*

[7] All this is said in connection with the infant's play with a woollen ball, with quaint suggestions that the singing tone accompanying the swinging like a ball affects the feelings, while the recognition of a change of position is a thing of "dawning thought," and that by tic-tac the movement is expressed. See *p. 176.*

[8] Dies fesselt die Sinnen- und Geistesthätigkeit des Kindes und gibt *ihm* mehrseitige Nahrung.

[9] In der Mitte seiner wahrnehmenden (empfindenden) seiner wirkenden und schaffenden, seiner vergleichenden (denkenden) Thätigkeit.

[10] Die Ausbildung der verschiedenen Richtungen der Geisteskraft des Kindes.

[11] "Journal of Education." Reprinted in "Child Life," January, 1901.

[12] "Analytic Psychology," Vol. I, *p. 152 et seq.*

[13] "Analytic Psychology," Vol. I, *p. 153.*

[14] It is true that Professor Stout complains of the loose way in which the word "activity" has been used, and that he is careful to define his own meaning, but Froebel too is careful. See Appendix I.

[15] See also *p. 82.*

[16] "Analytic Psychology," Vol. II, *p. 82.*

[17] "The Conception of Immortality," *p. 58.*

[18] Froebel is comparing the child with other young animals, and somewhat scornfully refers to those who, "notwithstanding the early manifestation of the instinct to employ himself," regard the human infant as inferior to the young of other animals.

[19] See chapter on Instinct.

[20] "In dem ersten Sinnenspiele, kommen also dem Kinde durch Wahrnehmen u. Schauen, durch Kommen, Bleiben u. Schwinden, durch Wechsel, also auch in gewisser Hinsicht durch frühes dunkles auffassen … somit von dunkler Vergleichung, die ersten Eindrücke der Seele, gleichsam die ersten Erkenntnisse zugleich durch Selbst-thätigkeit, wie durch die sein Leben und dessen Forderungen in sich tragende Mutterliebe."—*P., p. 66.*

[21] It does not, however, follow that this outer object, or this manner of presenting it, is so important as Froebel supposed; see Chapter IX.

[22] See *p. 66.*

[23] See Chapter II.

[24] "Principles of Psychology," Vol. II, *p. 884.*

[25] Froebel is too often ignorantly accused of being "soft," but it is a mistake to think that he leaves fear out of count. What he insists on is, that rightly used authority should produce self-control, not servility.

[26] See *p. 90.*

[27] Macmillan, 1906.

[28] *P. 53.*

[29] "Social Psychology," *p. 61.*

[30] Mr. McDougall allows (*p. 60*) that in the case of an unprovoked blow, the impulse, the thwarting of which provokes anger, is the impulse of self-assertion.

[31] For example, on *p. 46*, "Hence language provides special names for such modes of affective experience, names such as anger, fear, curiosity"; and on *p. 94*, in connection with the sympathetic induction of emotion, we have, "Later still, fear, curiosity, and, I think, anger are communicated readily from one child to another"; and there are other examples.

[32] *P. 51.*

[33] This is all that can be said, for the passage seems incomplete; after "entwickelt … der Trieb die Neigung," comes only "sie führen zur Gemüths- und Herzensbildung; und aus ihr geht in dem Knaben Geistes- und Willensthätigkeit hervor."

[34] For a fuller account of these "Gifts," see Chap. VIII., *p. 148.*

[35] In the well-known translation by F. and E. Lord:
"You wonder why a game at hide-and-seek Brings a glad flush of joy to baby's cheek? The sense of his own personality Is causing all this joy that you can see When people call him, say, 'Where's Baby been?' He feels that it is he, himself, they mean."

[36] "Social Psychology," *p. 89.*

[37] "The Play of Man," *p. 400.*

[38] "The Play of Man," *p. 382.*

[39] See *p. 194.*

[40] In another place Froebel does say that, "Only on condition that the genuine spirit of play—i.e. the true spirit of life—lives in the teacher, can he call it forth in the child."

[41] See Appendix II.

[42] See *pp. 93, 94.*

[43] See *p. 43.*

[44] Froebel goes on to say: "I believe, that after progressing through the vast orbit of almost two generations (he was nearly fifty-nine) I have been carried round to the point of commencement, to the fountain head of the education of mankind, but *with the significant addition of a full consciousness of my task.*"

[45] The material can of course be used at any age provided it conveys suitable ideas in a suitable manner. Some of it is even now found useful in helping senior classes to realize problems in area and in volume.

[46] Many years ago, a young teacher came to me for help. She had been told to give her class number lessons, for a whole term, from Gift III, which consists of eight little cubes, and the children had long since grasped 4 + 4, 6 + 2, 5 + 3, and 8 - 4, 8 - 2, etc. I suggested that she should leave the number out and let the children play with the blocks. "Oh! I mayn't do that," was the answer, "they have building with Gift IV."

[47] A really pathetic story has been told me of an earnest teacher in far Australia, whose educational opportunities had been very limited, but whose desire for knowledge was most sincere. She had been listening without comprehension to some glib user of phrases, and was bewailing her ignorance to an enlightened teacher who knew there had been little of real value, and who said with a laugh "Never mind, Miss ——, it is only a case of 'Mind and Matter glide swift into the vortex of immensity.'" And the listener said, "Oh please, would you say that slowly, and I'll write it down."

[48] These objections were embodied in a paper entitled "A Criticism of Froebelian Pedagogy," which Mr. Graham Wallas read at a Conference of the Froebel Society in January 1901, and which was published in the Conference Supplement for Child Life, July 1901.

[49] See *p. 200.*

[50] Few critics are likely to go so far as Mr. Winch, who gave as a Froebelian conception "that the true destiny of man is to be obtained by gratifying every youthful impulse." But, Mr. Winch is perhaps not to be taken seriously, for in the same paper he took *one sentence out of a passage on the importance of continuity extending over four pages*, and says of it, "This jerky discontinuity (!) has not the slightest support in biological science, and never had." (See Memorandum written for Mr. Graham Wallas in "Problems of Education.")

[51] Deshalb sollen Erziehung, Unterricht und Lehre ursprünglich und in ihren ersten Grundzügen nothwendig leidend, nachgehend (nur behütend schützend), nicht vorschreibend, bestimmend, eingreifend sein.

[52] Mr. Graham Wallas said: "The educational task for us is not to find out how completely we can stand aside, but how far we can so influence the environment of the child, as to cause those tendencies in it which we think best, to become permanent."

[53] Mr. Graham Wallas said: "From the beginning of the Darwinian reconstruction of the moral sciences, it was absurd, while speaking of 'environment,' to ignore the fact that the deliberate care and contrivance of the parent must form a large part of the environment of the child." The passage quoted shows that Froebel was guilty of no such absurdity.

[54] "Is Development from Within?" "Child Life," October, 1904, and January, 1905.

[55] See *p. 192.*

[56] "Second Review of Plays: A Fragment," but part of this has been omitted in the English translation.

[57] Those who desire a full and scholarly account of Froebel's philosophy are referred to that given by Professor Angus MacVannel, Ph.D., "Teachers' College Record," Vol. IV, No. 5. The Macmillan Co., New York.

[58] In Gottes Welt, eben weil es die Welt Gottes, durch Gott Gewordenes ist, spricht sich ein Stetiges, das heisst ungetrennt Fortgehendes der Entwickelung in Allem und durch Alles aus.

[59] See Appendix, *p. 216.*

[60] "Das Pedagogik des Kindergartens," *p. 329.*

[61] According to this principle, the mere fact that a particle is moving with a certain velocity in a certain direction, is in itself a reason why it should continue to move with the same velocity in the same direction…. Now, in so far as continuance of change in a certain direction is traceable to the pre-existence of change in that direction, this whole process may be regarded as being in a perfectly intelligible sense, self-determining ("Analytic Psychology," Vol. I, *p. 146*).

[62] "Analytic Psychology," Vol. I, *p. 147.*

[63] "Analytic Psychology," Vol. I, *p. 168.*

[64] "Analytic Psychology," Vol. I, *p. 155.*

[65] "Analytic Psychology," Vol. I, *p. 156.*

[66] "Analytic Psychology," Vol. I, *p. 156.*

[67] *P. 191.*

[68] And so to regard "each successive moment of the world-process as issuing out of the preceding by purely immanent casuality."

[69] "Analytic Psychology," Vol. I, *p. 156.*

[70] "Unity and Froebel are synonymous terms," is one "howler" from a student's examination paper.

[71] Ed. by Development, *p. 212.*

[72] "The Eternal Life," *p. 14.*

[73] "Das Kindergartenwesen," *p. 330.*

www.ingramcontent.com/pod-product-compliance
Lightning Source LLC
Chambersburg PA
CBHW081402280526
45788CB00009B/2962